Anti-inflammatory diet guide

A comprehensive guide for the Anti-inflammatory diet plan, with healthy and tasty recipes to revitalize your life by losing weight and reducing long-term illness.

[Tony Cook]

Anti-inflammatory diet guide

Book Description   15

INTRODUCTION   17

Chapter 1: What is Inflammation?   19

Chapter 2: T of Inflammation?   23

Chapter 3: Myths, misconceptions and mistakes made by
individuals   26

Chapter 4: How Dieting works   40

Chapter 5: An overview of Anti-Inflammatory Diet   43

Chapter 6: Weight Loss and the Importance of Calories   64

Chapter 7: Planning a proper diet plan   69

Chapter 8: Balancing your Calorie intake   72

Chapter 9: Breakfast Recipes   76

   Zucchini and Sprout Breakfast Mix   76

   Tomato and Olive Salad   77

   Blueberry and Cashew Mix   78

   Easy Almond Zucchini Bowl   79

   Sweet Potato Hash   80

   Zucchini Breakfast Salad   81

   Quinoa and Spinach Breakfast Salad   82

   Carrots Breakfast Mix   83

   Avocado Omelet   84

   Italian Breakfast Salad   85

Broccoli and Squash Mix _____ 86

Greens and Berries Mix _____ 87

Veggie and Eggs _____ 88

Coconut Pear Bowl _____ 89

Breakfast Corn Salad _____ 90

Simple Basil Tomato Mix _____ 91

Cucumber and Avocado Salad _____ 92

Watermelon Salad _____ 92

Coconut Porridge _____ 93

Blackberry and Strawberry Salad _____ 94

Breakfast Kale Frittata _____ 95

Cranberry Granola Bars _____ 96

Spinach and Berry Smoothie _____ 97

Chapter 10: Lunch Recipes _____ 98

Tasty Grilled Asparagus _____ 98

Easy Roasted Carrots _____ 99

Oven Roasted Asparagus _____ 99

Squash Side Salad _____ 100

Colored Iceberg Salad _____ 102

Fennel Side Salad _____ 103

Corn Mix _____ 104

Persimmon Side Salad _____ 105

Roast green beans with cranberries _____ 106

Roasted cheesy mushrooms _____ 107

Herbed Pork _____ 108

Garlic Pork Shoulder 109

Pork and Creamy Veggie Sauce 110

Ground Pork Pan 111

Tarragon Pork Steak 113

Pork Meatballs 114

Nutmeg Meatballs Curry 115

Pan seared sausage and kale 116

Pan-Fried Chorizo Mix 117

Pork Rolls 118

Salad Bowl of CapreseWith Tomato 120

Sauté Cabbage with Butter 121

Saute Edamame with Mint 122

Sauteed Broccoli with Parmesan 123

Sautéed Kohlrabi with Parsley 124

Sautéed Mixed Vegetable with Pumpkin Seeds 125

Side Cauliflower Salad 126

Spicy Green Beans and Vinaigrette 127

Stuffed Sausage with Bacon Wrappings 129

Tasty Lunch Pizza 130

Turkey and Collard Greens Soup 131

Warm Delicious Roasted Olives 133

Yummy Creamy Spaghetti Pasta: Side Dish 134

Yummy Muffins 135

Zucchini and Squash Noodles with Peppers 136

Baked Potato Mix 137

Spicy Brussels sprouts 139

Baked Cauliflower 140

Baked Broccoli 141

Easy Slow Cooked Potatoes 142

Mashed Potatoes 143

Avocado Side Salad 144

Classic Side Dish Salad 145

Easy Kale Mix 146

Asparagus Salad 147

Green Side Salad 148

Baked Zucchini 149

Chapter 11 : Dinner Recipes 151

Biryani 151

Autumn Roasted Green Beans 152

Zoodles 154

Roasted Rosemary Potatoes 155

Sweet Potato Wedges 156

Best Lentil Curry 157

Parmesan sprinkled garlic beans 158

Lamb & Pineapple Kebabs 159

Baked Meatballs & Scallions 160

Roasted Brussels Sprouts 162

Pork with Bell Pepper 163

Roasted Summer Squash 164

Savory Baked Acorn Squash 165

Pork with Pineapple 166

Caraway Pork Mix _____ 168

Roasted Mixed Olives _____ 169

Rolls of Sausage Pizzas _____ 170

Lamb Burgers with Avocado Dip _____ 171

Mustard Pork Chops _____ 173

Greek Mixed Roasted Vegetables _____ 174

Pork and Lentils Soup _____ 176

Pork and Veggies Stew _____ 177

Pork and Snow Peas Salad _____ 179

Pork and Beans Stew _____ 180

Spiced Pork _____ 181

Pork Chili _____ 183

Ground Pork with Water Chestnuts _____ 185

Glazed Pork chops with Peach _____ 187

Pork chops in Creamy Sauce _____ 189

Baked Pork & Mushroom Meatballs _____ 190

Chapter 12: Snacks Recipes _____ 192

Chickpeas and Pepper Hummus _____ 192

Lemony Chickpeas Dip _____ 193

Chili Nuts _____ 194

Protein Bars _____ 195

Eggplant, Olives and Basil Salad _____ 196

Fresh Tomato, Onion and Jalapeno Pepper Salsa __ 197

Fresh Veggie Bars _____ 198

Green Beans And Avocado with Chopped Cilantro __ 199

Italian Pizza Dip   200

Jalapeno Cheesy Balls   202

Keto Veggie Noodles: Side Dish   203

Minty Zucchini Rolls   204

Sesame Zucchini Spread   205

Shrimp Salad with Tomato and Radish   206

Shrimp wrapped with prosciutto   207

Simple Tomato Tarts   208

Special Tomato AndBocconcini: Side Dish   210

Stir-Fried Queso   211

Potato Chips   212

Peach Dip   213

Cereal Mix   214

Easy Tuna Cakes   215

Mushrooms Stuffed with shrimp mixture.   216

Oven-baked Crackers   217

Parmesan Spinach Balls   218

Pecan with Maple syrup Bars   219

Plum and Jalapeno Salad with Basil   221

Seasoned Easy Fried Cabbage   222

Tasty Avocado Spread   223

Red Pepper Muffins   224

Nuts and Seeds Mix   225

Tortilla Chips   226

Kale Chips   227

Pan-Fried Cheesy Sticks   227

546. Pan-fried Italian Meatballs 228

Parmesan Basil Dip 230

Parmesan Chicken Wings 230

Chapter 13: Healthy and Delicious Beverages 233

Citrus Flavored Water 233

Basil-Infused Tomato Water 234

Refreshing Strawberry 234

Grapefruit Water 235

Black Lemon Iced Tea 235

Raspberries Iced Tea 236

Chamomile Orange Iced Tea 237

Mint Tea 238

Basil Ginger Tea 238

Green Veggie Juice 239

Pineapple Juice 239

CONCLUSION 241

Legal & Disclaimer

The information contained in this book and its contents is not designed to replace or take the place of any form of medical or professional advice; and is not meant to replace the need for independent medical, financial, legal or other professional advice or services, as may be required. The content and information in this book has been provided for educational and entertainment purposes only.

The content and information contained in this book has been compiled from sources deemed reliable, and it is accurate to the best of the Author's knowledge, information and belief. However, the Author cannot guarantee its accuracy and validity and cannot be held liable for any errors and/or omissions. Further, changes are periodically made to this book as and when needed. Where appropriate and/or necessary, you must consult a professional (including but not limited to your doctor, attorney, financial advisor or such other professional advisor) before using any of the suggested remedies, techniques, or information in this book.

Upon using the contents and information contained in this book, you agree to hold harmless the Author from and against any damages, costs, and expenses, including any legal fees potentially resulting from the application of any of the information provided by this book. This disclaimer applies to any loss, damages or injury caused by the use and application, whether directly or indirectly, of any advice or information presented, whether for breach of contract, tort, negligence, personal injury, criminal intent, or under any other cause of action.

You agree to accept all risks of using the information presented inside this book.

You agree that by continuing to read this book, where appropriate and/or necessary, you shall consult a professional (including but not limited to your doctor, attorney, or financial advisor or such other advisor as needed) before using any of the suggested remedies, techniques, or information in this book.

Book Description

Inflammation can hijack our feelings of wellness and slow us down, but when it becomes chronic, this may signal that something is out of alignment in our diet or lifestyle. Normal inflammation occurs in the body on a regular basis as part of our natural process of maintaining a healthy internal balance. It's only when the necessary process of inflammation gets out of hand that well-being can become impaired.

We'll also present the principles of an easy anti-inflammatory diet, based on whole foods and grounded in science, to support you in restoring your natural balance. Our simple lists of foods to include (and those to avoid) will help you choose meals far beyond the recipes. We'll also touch on how people's bodies respond differently to particular ingredients, so you can personalize these recipes to best meet your own nutritional needs.

The more difficult side of this equation is that the visceral fat is not one that ever truly leaves the body. It is the fat that hides out in all of the nooks and crannies of your abdominal organs, which makes it dangerous to remove with such invasive procedures as liposuction. Neither will these fat cells dissipate from your body with weight loss and exercise. However, as you reduce obesity levels, these fat cells respond by reducing in size, and that reduction slows down the production of as many harmful, inflammatory chemicals.

INTRODUCTION

A good and healthy diet can do miracles no medicine in this world can do. With a good diet, you can ensure a disease-free life with active metabolism. Our body goes through a constant process of self-repairment and experiences various phenomenon on the way.

Inflammations are therefore a temporary process of regeneration and reintegration of normal conditions following a damage; however, if the harmful agents persist or if there is a production of mainly type 1 cytokines, it can become chronic. In this case one can observe a progressive reduction of the microcirculation processes described above - as it happens during the recovery - while at the same time the infiltrated cells are progressively constituted by macrophages and lymphocytes that are frequently disposed around the vascular wall like a sleeve, which causes its compression. As a consequence, a state of tissue suffering is established, which is established by the presence of the infiltrate and by the reduction of blood flow caused by the vascular compression.

Inflammation is one of the body's responses to a number of environmental factors. The idea behind the conception of this book is to provide you with all the pros of opting a dietary approach to reduce or eliminate risks of inflammation and to make you aware of the relevant recipes. Let's get started!

Chapter 1: What is Inflammation?

When using the terms inflammation or phlogosis one intends the set of alterations that occur in an area of the organism that has been hit by a damage of an intensity that has not affected the vitality of all cells within the area. Such damage could be induced by physical agents (such as traumas or heat), chemical agents (such as toxic components or acids) and biological agents (such as bacteria and viruses).

The response to the damage, the inflammation in fact, is given by the cells that have survived it and is therefore primarily a local reaction. Medical terminology defines the reaction by adding -tis to the name of the organ that is inflamed (for example the terms tendinitis and hepatitis indicate, respectively, a tendon and liver inflammation). The reaction was defined as primarily local instead of exclusively local as several molecules that are synthesized and released by the cells that participate in the phenomenon move into the blood and operate on long distanced organs, especially the liver. Thus, stimulating the liver cells to release other substances that are responsible for the acute response phase to the inflammation. The presence of a fever and leucorrhoea (which is an increase in the number of leukocytes circulating in the blood) represent other systematic indications of phlogosis. The inflammation itself is a useful process to the organism, as it allows it to neutralize (if present) the agent that has caused damage, and reintegrate the normal condition pre-existing to the detrimental event.

In the case of muscular injury, for example, the inflammation process that follows is especially necessary to activate a subdivided process of the very own damage (in this case the agent generating the damage would be a physical agent, like a trauma, and there will be no necessity to eliminate the damaging agent, unlike in other cases).

The most known symptoms of inflammations are an increase in the local temperature, swelling, redness, soreness, and functional compromission. The phenomenons that cause such symptoms are mainly caused by events that involve the microcirculation of blood. An extremely rapid vasoconstriction is followed by the relaxation of the smooth muscular fiber cells present on terminal arterioles' walls, with resulting vasodilation and increasing blood flow to the traumatized area (which causes the increase in local temperature and redness). Subsequently, the higher blood flow stagnates in the traumatized zone, thus increasing the blood's viscosity (given by the red blood cells' aggregation and by the plasma's outflow to the intercellular junctions); leukocytes will also start flowing out the blood at the extravascular compartment where they are attracted by specific cytokines. Thus, the exudate is formed, which is the root of the swelling. It is constituted partly by a liquid and partly by suspended cells in it. Finally, the subdivided process of cellular damage will start.

The set of processes that is described above is mediated by various molecules which trigger, maintain and also limit the modifications in the microcirculation. Such molecules are called chemical mediators of phlogosis, and they can come from different sources and have different scopes. These are histamine, serotonin, arachidonic acid's metabolites (prostaglandines, leukotrienes and thromboxanes), lysosomal enzymes, type 1 and type 2 cytokines, nitric oxide, the kinin system and the complement system. Instead, the cells that intervene in the inflammatory processes are constituted by mastocytes, basophils, neutrophils and eosinophils, monocytes/macrophages, natural killer cells, platelets, lymphocytes, plasma cells, endothelial cells and fibroblasts.

Next, fibroblasts can be stimulated to proliferate, with the consequence that many chronic phlogosis cases culminate with an excessive formation of connective tissue which constitutes fibrosis or sclerosis. For example, that is the case for cellulite, a socially unaesthetic disease which affects many women, caused by the increase in volume of adipose cells in some areas of the body (mostly thighs and glutes) with the lack of liquid draining and the process of local inflammation which can induce, at the worst phases, fibrosis and sclerosis with the formation of micronodules which give skin the classic "orange peel" aspect.

The inflammation itself can therefore be defined as a "physiologic" response of the organism to a detrimental stimulus (for example a cut or a trauma) and it can be of the acute kind (angio phlogosis), mainly involving the modifications to the vascular system to ease the reparation of the damage and the inflow of the immune system cells, or it can be chronic, of long duration and with a persistent reaction by the immune system. During these processes, it was clear how chemical mediators are generated in great quantities, such as inflammatory cytokines, which not only have a local action in the damaged tissue but also flow throughout the whole body and "inflame" it in chronic conditions.

That is the case, for example, for the pathological alterations of the Intestinal Microbiome (see related chapter) or more generally of the intestinal barrier with the diffusion of material from the enteric lumen in the blood flow and generation of a low level chronic inflammatory state.

Over time such conditions can increase the risk of many metabolic pathologies like obesity, diabetes mellitus and metabolic syndrome. Here is why it is good to know how to "deinflammate" our organism also through our diet choices.

Chapter 2: T of Inflammation?

You should know the two major types of inflammation to better deal with it. These are:

Acute inflammation:

It is the instantaneous response of the body in the result of damage to body cells. Swelling occurs within 2 to 3 seconds of the injury. It doesn't persist for a longer duration.

Acute inflammation is one that starts quickly and becomes serious in a brief time. Signs or symptoms are normally just present for a couple of days and nights but may persist for a couple of weeks in some instances.

Systemic or Chronic inflammation:

It is a long-term inflammation, which is often caused due to allergies, cancer, diabetes, lungs diseases, asthma, heart complexities, etc. In these cases, the inflammation is cured only by treating the root cause.

Inflammation may be the defense reply that centers your immune system's consideration toward combating a perceived menace -- often microorganisms or Trojans or harm from international invaders, like poisons. When a section of your body becomes reddened, swollen, very hot and often agonizing, this is swelling in action.

Great up to now. But when swelling is chronically fired up, the immune system's capability to fight off different insects and pathogens will be compromised.

Chronic inflammation is frequently regarded as the effect of your "overactive" disease fighting capability -- as if your immune purpose is perplexed or malfunctioning. But can be this definitely what's going on? Or carry out we just reside in an increasingly harmful and stressful entire world?

After all, a lot of people today are confused with anxiety and environmental poisons, like endocrine-disrupting and cancer-causing substances from food to drinking water to household cleansers. And your body has every right to respond defensively. Foods allergies, poor diet program, toxins, and pressure are the most important culprits.

To combat irritation, we have to help our anatomies deal with this continuous harm of immune causes. One of the better ways to aid your body in combatting inflammation would be to consume an anti-inflammatory diet program.

Chapter 3: Myths, misconceptions and mistakes made by individuals

Your body's metabolism dictates your ability to produce energy. Metabolism is the process of breaking down food particles by the organic cells of your body. The metabolic process also plays a crucial role in your ability to burn fat to attain your ideal body weight.

Therefore, it is significant to your general health to have a high capacity of burning fat for energy. In short, it is always paramount to enhance your body's metabolic process.

Repeatedly, people are engaging in activities and behaviors. that are wrecking their metabolism.

Worse, they are unaware of it all! The anti-inflammatory diet directly refers to the metabolic processes and the immune system of your body. Hence, therein gushes forth most of the common mistakes, misunderstandings, and misconceptions of practicing the regimen.

Here is a compilation of the top mistakes while practicing the regimen. Learning these common errors will help you to avoid these glitches along the way. The list also includes the corresponding tips:

Misstep #1: Concentrating on Calories & Heedless on Hormones

One of the most misinterpreted myths misguiding many people is the assumption that the weight of the body bears a direct connection to the number of calories consumed. This outdated perception is an erroneous way of looking at how your body's metabolic functions. You should instead embrace the significant reality of linking your caloric consumptions with your hormonal and body functions. The reality is that the types of food that you consume can alter your hormones completely and hinder the efficiency of your metabolism to burn fat.

In other words, consuming a calorically similar regimen of refined carbs against low-glycemic indexed whole foods will produce different effects on your metabolic processes. Likewise, indulging in a low-carb diet compared to a high-carb diet will cause advantageous outcomes on how your cells will burn fat for fuel, regardless of your caloric intake.

Again, your hormones and metabolism operate beyond food consumption. Your five primary hormones, which control your fat-burning process, are insulin, leptin, ghrelin, cortisol, and adiponectin. An array of factors influences these hormones such as your regular exercise routines, sleep quality, stress levels, hydration levels, and diet.

☐ Myth-1: Curb Carbs, Fill Fats

– Lowering your carb intakes and increasing your consumption of healthy fats makes a great difference towards improving your metabolism. Such a regimen simultaneously helps to stabilize your blood sugar levels, decreases insulin levels, and boosts the burning of fats. Consuming a surplus of carbs tends to convert the excesses into fats, stored as fatty tissues. Their regular consumption characterizes typically a chronically high blood sugar level, which results in a diverse range of destructive effects on your body.

However, switching your body into a fat-burning machine is technically engaging with a low-carb and high fat (LCHF) diet. Research supports this dietary model since it outperforms a low-fat regimen in countering obesity, diabetes, and other inflammatory factors.

☐ Myth-2: Short & Strenuous Exercise Engagements – Your exercise habits significantly contribute to the general health of your hormones.

Many people indulge in daily exercises with the aim of losing weight in the wrong way. Low-intensity cardio workouts daily are harmful to your body and as such, unnecessary.

Instead, short-duration and high-intensity intermittent exercises (HIIE) are highly effective for hormone enhancement. Modern studies confirm that these more explosive modes of exercises provide increased benefits for shedding weight as opposed to other forms of exercises.

Among the more well-known examples of these workouts are those boxing sessions or 30-second sprints followed by an active recovery activity of 2 to 4 minutes (usually, walking or other forms of low-intensity body movements). If ever you deem such exercises as severely intensive for your body, then you can always modify them.

An ideal phase, to begin with, would be 30 seconds of performing each exercise program, followed by another 30 seconds of resting. You may also Adjust the exercise movements to make them less straining or comfortably easier.

Nonetheless, your aim should be pushing yourself to your limits of performing high-intensity exercises. Attaining this objective allows your body to adapt to an appropriate hormonal balance gained from these typical exercises.

☐ Myth-3: Terminate Toxic Substances & Supplies – Accumulated toxins in your body can directly lead to poor fat metabolism. For instance, in today's modern society, many food chemical components can mimic the functions of estrogen (a hormone promoting fat retention) with potentials for completely disrupting a hormonal balance.

You can prevent exposing your body to such risks by eating only wild-caught or pasture-raised meats and organically grown vegetables. Furthermore, avoid using beauty products, synthetic plastics, unfiltered water, and other similar supplies filled with toxic substances.

Always be aware of what you introduce to your body. Check and use only products that contain natural ingredients as much as possible.

Misstep #2: Mindless on Micronutrients

For most of us, we spend the majority our time focusing more on our consumptions of fats, proteins, and carbohydrates— the major macronutrients. Although the amount of each of these macronutrients is a vital factor for healthy nutrition planning, the number of micronutrients may disputably be more significant. Your body uses dozens of various beneficial micronutrient substances.

These micronutrients include vitamins, minerals, fatty acids, enzymes, antioxidants, and all sorts of essential compounds contained in foods. Their role is to keep you energized, produce hormones and digestive enzymes, repair and rejuvenate cells and tissues, mineralize bones, slow down oxidation damage or aging caused by free radicals, and prevent nutritional deficiencies. Deficiencies of specific micronutrients may lead to various health issues such as bone loss, thyroid problems,poor digestion, and mental impairment. Notably, a low level of micronutrient consumption influences your body's metabolism directly in a manner that promotes a major gain of fats.

For instance, nutrients such as zinc, selenium, and iodine serve to produce thyroid hormones. When you severely lack these nutrients, you may incur lower thyroid hormone productions and a much slower metabolism.

☐ Myth-1: Rainbow Ration Regimen – Various colors in diverse foods represent the presence of corresponding types of nutrients and unique benefits. For instance:

☐ Red Foods – are rich in carotenoids that are beneficial for your heart, eyes, immune system, blood, joints, and skin.

☐ Orange Foods – are excellent sources of fiber and vitamin C that promote collagen growth. They also contain cryptoxanthins— antioxidants that protect cells from damage and cancer growths.

☐ Purple & Blue Foods – are high in powerful anthocyanins— antioxidants that protect against heart disease, improve mineral absorption, enhance exercise performance, boost brain function, and other highly anti-inflammatory mechanisms. Purple and blue foods can even synergize well with a high-fat regimen to accelerate fat burning.

☐ Green Foods – contain trace minerals, chlorophyll, and sets of the B-vitamins and Vitamin K that detoxify your body, fight free radicals, and improve your immune system.

In particular, green foods are leafy greens, which are ideal inclusions to low-carb nutrition that support fat metabolism.

☐ Yellow Foods – possess antioxidant compounds that convert into vitamins C, B6, and A, potassium, phosphorus, riboflavin, fiber, magnesium, and folate. All these help to improve your heart functions, vision, digestive, and immune systems.

☐ White Foods – have lots of vitamins, minerals, and other vital food nutrients that your body needs to maintain a healthy weight and to protect against various inflammatory diseases.

☐ Myth-2: Mineral Maintenance – Your body requires both major and minor trace minerals to maintain optimum wellness. These minerals are necessary for your enzymes to function appropriately apart from supporting essential metabolic processes such as thyroid hormone production.

Generally, the required amount of trace minerals for your body should be less than 100 milligrams a day. The key trace elements are zinc, selenium, molybdenum, manganese, iron, iodine, copper, cobalt, and chromium.

They are nature's catalysts that stimulate the work of enzymes, which further generate all metabolic processes necessary for life.

Deficiencies in mineral intake disable your body to gain adequate energy, proper bone formation, blood circulation and maintain optimal levels of hormone production. Excellent sources of minerals include the following:

☐ Avocados

☐ Fermented Foods

☐ Ghee or Grass-Fed Butter

☐ Grass-Fed Meats

☐ Leafy Greens

☐ Olives

☐ Pasture-Raised Eggs

☐ Pink Salts

☐ Sea Vegetables

☐ Vegetable or Bone Broth

☐ Wild-Caught Fish

☐ Myth-3: Staple Supplements – Myopic or careless farming practices have resulted in poor soil conditions in several areas of the world. For this reason, it becomes more unreliable to determine whether farm products or the foods you eat contain proper levels of nutrients, which they should. Therefore, having a staple of daily food supplements is essential.

To cover all of your bases, an excellent strategy is to consume multi-vitamins, multi-minerals, or all-in-one superfoods. You do not necessarily need to take all these in one sitting, but consuming at least one of them is highly advisable, especially if you are nutrient-deficient.

A huge mistake most people commit is to leave their digestive problems unaddressed, particularly when trying to figure out their metabolism issues. Thus, if you are experiencing any digestive issues like leaky gut or dysbiosis (gut bacterial imbalance), reduced stomach acids, and small intestinal bacterial overgrowth (SIBO), then it is difficult for your body to regulate hunger, much less, absorb all the food nutrients.

Furthermore, your body will have a sluggish metabolism that will leave you overweight and feeling lethargic. Poor digestion may also cause an undesirable spiral of effects that stifle your metabolism and thyroid hormone conversion.

Misstep #3: Availing Needlessly Anti-Nutrients

Anti-nutrients either deplete or prevent absorption of other useful nutrients in your body. They may manifest in various forms such as the following:

☐ Toxins – heighten the demand for detoxifying the liver. The delicate detoxification process requires the involvement of various multiple nutrients. These nutrients somehow include food products that contain antibiotics, artificial sweeteners, heavy metals,herbicides, pesticides, and other chemical elements within or on them.

The most common types of these toxic anti-nutrients are non-organic foods and processed vegetable oils. Both food items highly tend to contain pesticides, which damage your gut and deplete nutrients from your body.

Processed vegetable oils do not provide your body with a source of fuel. Besides, they are highly inflammatory. The more you consume them, the more you should eat consume omega-3 fats just to offset the harmful effects.

☐ Sugars –stimulate the process of glycolysis (breaking down sugars and carbohydrates), thus causing high sugar levels in the blood. These processes deplete vitamins B, C, and D, as well as calcium, chromium, and magnesium minerals in your body.

When consumed in excess, sugars may even lead to disruptions in cellular energy production. In effect, energy deficiencies slow down the protective mechanisms of metabolism.

☐ Phytates, Lectins, and Oxalates – are plant-based anti-nutrient proteins and compounds. People are often unaware of eating them because they are essential constituents of many everyday food items.

Plants are immobile and unable to protect themselves from various predators by either a 'fight or flight' response. Instead, they create compounds— phytates, lectins, and oxalates— that are micro toxins or poisonous for their predators.

☐ Myth-1: Avoid Anti-Nutrients Necessarily – Limiting your intakes of anti-nutrients requires you to know their chief origins. For instance, phytates generally come from legumes, grains, and nuts. While phytates are healthy for your body, they constrict the absorption of minerals such as zinc, magnesium, and calcium. Oxalates are commonly present in beets, cacao, nuts, raspberries, seeds, and spinach. Lectins are predominant in nightshade vegetables, seeds, nuts, legumes, and grains.

You do not need to avoid them altogether, but it is prudent to lessen your consumptions of these plant-based anti-nutrients. Otherwise, you will eventually incur serious gut health issues, chronic pain, or kidney problems.

☐ Myth-2: Soaking & Steaming Preparation Procedures – To further augment the reduction of anti-nutrient content in some foods, you should practice soaking seeds and nuts in filtered water right on the eve before you use or consume them.

Some nuts and seeds may sprout after soaking them. These processes of soaking and sprouting unveil a higher nutritional profile, making the nuts and seeds more suitable for your digestive tract.

Raw cruciferous (mustard family) of vegetables can be direct sources of anti-nutrients, which pose difficulties on your digestive tract. A better way to lessen the disabling effects of these typical vegetables is to steam them before eating. Steaming also serves to break down exterior cellulose fibers gently, and thus, making it easier for your digestive tract system to process. Fermenting is also another viable option.

Misstep #4: Treating Thirst as Hydrating Hunger

Mostly, people easily misinterpret thirst for hunger. Yet the reality is that a dehydrated body can convey a false signal to your brain, indicating a low blood sugar and prompt you to eat.

If you are engaging in a low-carb dietary plan and frequently end up feeling hungry between meals, then, you are either dehydrated or not eating enough fats. Hence, instead of grabbing immediately for a snack, drink a glass of water first and observe how you feel.

☐ Myth-1: Win Wellness with Water – Hydration is crucial on any dietary program. However, there are several recommendations for adequate water intake.

Studies note that all it takes to impair your physical performances is a water loss equivalent to 2% of your body weight. A water loss of roughly 2.8% of your body weight can reduce your cognitive functions. By these conclusions, it is vital to reiterate how your ideal water intake directly relates to your body weight.

As a basic guideline, your daily minimum water intake should be half of your total body weight (based in pounds) in ounces of water. Ideally, you should consume ¾ of your entire body weight in ounces of water per day. This recommendation is highly unlikely if you weigh more than 3,000 pounds. Nevertheless, if you are slim and lean, this advice is simple to follow as long as you stay hydrated between meals.

Applying baseline values, consider drinking more to refill the water lost from exercising. The same studies suggest that for water lost due to exercises, you should drink a half-liter (18-ounces) of water for each pound of your total body weight.

Hence, drinking water amidst your diet demands you to weigh yourself daily. This procedure allows you to know how much weight you have already lost or what weight you should ideally maintain.

Nonetheless, one of the more popular hydration strategies is to hydrate your body early in the day. For instance, drinking 1-2 liters (16-32 ounces) of water before taking your first meal is an excellent way of cleansing the body, promoting better digestion, and restoring dehydration that has just occurred overnight.

In addition, proper hydration of your body is dependent on both water and mineral contents.

Combining a pinch of sea salt with your water is a bright idea to add electrolytes— body minerals found in the bloodstream, tissues, urine, and other body fluids that help to balance water retention in your body

Adding organic acids (i.e., citric and acetic acids) in your water is also a great way to improve your body's hydration and stabilize your blood sugar level. You can consume these acids in the form of lemon juice (citric acid) or apple cider vinegar (acetic acid). You only have to add a splash of either organic acids to your water to curtail your cravings until mealtime.

Chapter 4: How Dieting works

Inflammation has always been a therapeutic secret, yet now it has turned into a foe of long haul health. Additional red platelets, safe cells, and antioxidants are hurrying to the injured site to recuperate it. In any case, conveyed excessively thus far,inflammation can be lethal, as when somebody is too scorched to even consider recovering.

Just in a couple that is previous of, has it unfolded that low-level incessant inflammation, which ordinarily goes unnoticed, has an influence on numerous life disorders, for example, hypertension, heart disease, cancer, and Alzheimer's disease.

The moderate trickle, dribble of inflammatory markers, can take a very long time to make real impedance, which implies that every individual must tailor his way of life to counter them. Diet alone is not sufficient to keep ceaseless, intense inflammation under control... yet it is a decent start. The Mediterranean diet has been known to help lessen inflammation in the body, so it is an incredible way to kick-start your diet. By embracing an anti-inflammatory diet, you go for two positive outcomes: keeping the microorganisms in your digestive tracts healthy and flourishing, thereby avoiding the drainage of lethal synthetics into the circulation system. There is additionally the circuitous benefit that a healthy stomach related framework, sends a sign of prosperity along the vagus nerve to the heart and cerebrum. There is a huge number of microorganisms that possess the intestinal tract, and are a fundamental piece of our complete DNA, contributing a great many separate genomes. Together this tremendous settlement is known as the microbiome. Here are some basic focuses to know. The gut microbiome is not the same as a culture to culture.

In every one of us, it is always moves accordingly to the diet, yet to pressure and even feelings. Because of its hereditary, multifaceted nature, an "ordinary" gut microbiome has not been characterized at this point. It is accepted that flourishing, healthy gut microbiome is

established on a wide scope of common foods wealthy in fruits, vegetables, and fiber. The cutting edge Western diet, which is low in fiber, yet high in sugar, salt, fat, and handling food, might be genuinely debasing the gut microbiome. At the point when the gut microbiome is harmed or debased, microscopic organisms start to discharge supposed endotoxins— the results of microbial activity. If these poisons spill through the intestinal divider into the circulatory system, markers for inflammation are activated, and persevere until the poisons are never again present.

Chapter 5: An overview of Anti-Inflammatory Diet

How Inflammation Helps—and Harms

When the immune system is working properly, inflammation plays an important role in our body's healthy response to injury or infection. Upon injury or infection, such as a scrape on the knee or exposure to the cold everyone else has at the office, our immune system rallies to restore health. This leads to a period of acute inflammation, which promotes healing as the body's defensive process repairs and restores integrity. Once the problem has been successfully managed, the immune response deactivates, and the inflammation around the area of injury or infection subsides.

When you notice that a paper cut on your finger is red, swollen, warm, and painful, this is all part of inflammation, which is taking place as a result of a smoothly running immune system. Immune cells have been activated to the site of the problem, so blood flow in the area increases, leading to the experience of swelling and heat, which will subside as the wound heals. Soon you'll have nothing to remember the paper cut by but a thin line of scar tissue. This kind of acute, localized inflammation may not require any additional treatment; however, maintaining a consistent anti-inflammatory diet like the one described in this book will ensure that your body has all the nutrients needed to support even this minor healing process.

Conversely, a little cut that seems to hang on too long, remaining puffy and painful and not making much progress in healing, might indicate a bigger issue. In this case, the normal process of acute inflammation may have continued unchecked, signaling a chronic inflammation that is more problematic. This can occur as a result of an unhealed infection like hepatitis B or C, prolonged exposure to environmental toxins like cigarette smoke, or existing health conditions like obesity or autoimmune disease. Lifestyle factors such as diet and stress can also amplify the inflammatory response. At first, there may not be any obvious symptoms of this kind of ongoing low-grade inflammation, yet in the long term, chronic inflammation can increase risk for or exacerbate a variety of diseases.

ANTI-INFLAMMATORY DIET GUIDELINES

Smart Dietary Choices

A whole foods approach to eating is the best route to decreasing inflammation, and that's the strategy we present here. As the benefits of anti-inflammatory diets become clearer, a growing number of studies reveal which foods are best to include or avoid as you move toward vibrant wellness. Let's check them out.

Foods That Fight Inflammation

FRUITS AND VEGETABLES. Consider yourself free to enjoy a wide range of fruits and vegetables on the anti-inflammatory diet—they're all good! Plant foods deliver a high-nutrient, low-calorie foundation and add bright, tempting color to any plate. These foods are a source of satisfying, anti-inflammatory fiber, plus vitamins, minerals, and micronutrients. Fruits and vegetables also contain powerful antioxidant compounds that help prevent cellular damage.

Berries, watermelon, apples, and pineapple in particular are proven anti-inflammatory superstars, thanks to their high levels of phytonutrients. Thousands of these chemicals can be found in different combinations in plant foods, and while they protect the plant against environmental damage, they also protect you on a cellular level, especially when you eat a wide range of produce. Citrus fruits provide high-antioxidant vitamin C, a knockout inflammation fighter. Vegetables such as onions, broccoli, and leafy greens support resistance to inflammation. Garlic and onion don't just add pungent flavor—they've also been studied extensively for their immune system benefits.

NIGHTSHADES. Beware the boundless Internet (mis)information available—some is inaccurate and not well grounded in science. Rumors that you can't enjoy nightshades such as tomatoes, potatoes, bell peppers, and eggplant on an anti-inflammatory diet are unfounded for most people. While some with autoimmune conditions like rheumatoid arthritis choose to avoid these nutritious vegetables, the Arthritis Foundation notes that no scientific data supports this, and in fact, the group cites research that shows that consumption of yellow and purple potatoes may actually lower inflammation. However, you are the expert of your own body. If you find that this restriction is supportive of your own health and well-being, then just try to include a wide range of other vegetables to ensure you are providing all the nutrition your body needs to heal. For most people, nightshade vegetables are part of a nutritious, anti-inflammatory diet. For instance, compounds such as the lycopene provided by cooked tomatoes make these vegetables standouts for fighting inflammation.

WHOLE AND ANCIENT GRAINS. Whole and ancient grains don't merely replace refined grains. They provide exciting flavors and textures, along with fiber, micronutrients, antioxidants, and protein. Naturally gluten-free grains, such as quinoa and amaranth, keep meals interesting and can be enjoyed by everyone.

GOOD FATS. We have learned that it's more important to enjoy the right kinds of fats in moderation than to try to eliminate fat altogether. Olive oil is a rich source of polyphenols, which are compounds shown to reduce indicators of inflammation, and it should be your primary cooking oil. Specialty oils like walnut oil or pumpkin seed oil add rich flavor and beneficial unsaturated fats. And we're happy to promote the benefits of dark chocolate, a delicious source of protective polyphenols—and a fine end to a meal!

OMEGA-3 FATTY ACIDS ARE ALL-STAR ANTI-INFLAMMATORY FATS. Include foods with this type of unsaturated fat frequently to optimize your whole diet approach. Fatty fish like salmon and sardines are excellent sources, as are some plant foods such as walnuts and flaxseed. Flaxseed may sound foreign, but it's been around for thousands of years, just now gaining popularity for its abundant fiber, protein, and powerful antioxidants called lignans. Consumption of flaxseed protects against inflammation and some cancers, but go for the ground version, so your body can absorb all that goodness. Seeds like hemp and chia are similarly helpful, as are pine nuts, which are actually nutrient-dense seeds.

HERBS AND SPICES. With countless options, each herb and spice has a unique profile of antioxidants and bright flavors to complement all kinds of cuisine. Turmeric deserves special mention for its proven anti-inflammatory and neuroprotective properties. Ginger, saffron, and cinnamon are other potent flavor enhancers worth trying. Herbs such as basil, rosemary, and thyme all have inflammation-fighting compounds, and their aroma and taste elevate the meal experience.

PROBIOTICS AND PREBIOTICS. What are these, anyway? Probiotics and prebiotics support immune and digestive health. Fermented foods such as yogurt, sauerkraut, pickles, tempeh, and kimchi are known as probiotic foods because they provide a direct infusion of healthy bacteria to your system in addition to their characteristic tang. Prebiotics are foods that feed those good gut bacteria—sources include high-fiber vegetables, whole grains, and beans. Cooked beans like black beans, chickpeas, and lentils also double as lean, plant-based proteins.

HEALTHY DRINKS. Washing foods down with kombucha keeps the probiotic theme going, although not everyone appreciates the sour taste of this fermented beverage! Thankfully, unsweetened teas are good beverage options—green tea is a particularly robust source of antioxidants. Drip coffee provides fiber and is one of the biggest contributors of antioxidants to the American diet—just try to keep it sugar-free. A glass of red wine from time to time provides protective resveratrol. Water is always a great choice for hydration and promotes the body's ability to detoxify at the cellular level.

OWN YOUR WATER

Water can be the most refreshing treat when you're parched. A decanter of water with sliced cucumber in a hotel lobby is a welcome sight to weary travelers. Yet it's amazing to see how many people have a hard time taking in enough water each day. If you're one of them, consider adding some fruits or herbs to your water to boost the flavor and the benefits. Buy a pretty glass pitcher; it will make the water look especially inviting. Ginger, thyme, basil, and rosemary make good herbal anti-inflammatory add-ins; beneficial fruits include orange, grapefruit, lemon, lime, apples, watermelon, and pineapple. Try water infused with blueberries and lemon, cucumber and mint, or beets and rosemary—or come up with your own favorite flavor combinations!

Foods That Worsen Inflammation

PROCESSED FOODS. There is no shortage of delicious, nourishing food to enjoy on your anti-inflammatory diet. To maximize the benefits, you'll want to leave behind those highly processed, packaged foods, as they are typically full of proinflammatory sodium, saturated fats, added sugars, and refined grains such as white flour or white rice.

AVOID ADDED SUGARS AND REFINED GRAINS FROM ANY SOURCE. These proinflammatory foods dramatically increase blood sugar, have more calories than they do nutrition, and are linked to many negative health effects.

PROCESSED AND RED MEAT. Some meats, such as ham and many deli meats, are highly processed and contain undesirable saturated fat and sodium. Red meat is another food to choose less frequently. Even lean cuts are likely to have high levels of proinflammatory saturated fats. You might be surprised to know that you should save backyard cookouts for special occasions. This is because fatty proteins like beef prepared with high-heat dry cooking methods increase production of proinflammatory substances called advanced glycation end products, or AGEs. Consider using lower-heat, moist cooking methods, such as stewing, sautéing, or poaching, to minimize this effect. Select lean, grass-fed beef options that offer protective omega-3s, in contrast with regular beef, which is high in proinflammatory omega-6 fats.

Foods to Consider with Care

Many foods fall in the middle of the health spectrum—these foods are neither the foundation of an anti-inflammatory diet nor the worst choices. These should be considered with care, depending on your own goals and current health condition. These foods are used sparingly in our recipes, and when we do include them, we offer substitutions.

CERTAIN OILS. A few plant-based oils should be approached thoughtfully. Corn, safflower, sunflower, and soy oils are high in proinflammatory omega-6s. Despite the trendiness of coconut oil on websites that promise "magic results" from consuming it in high amounts, it is a highly saturated fat, and there is no reason to believe it is healthy to consume in excess. Occasional dishes can be prepared with coconut oil, but keep olive oil as your go-to kitchen staple.

SKIN-ON DARK-MEAT POULTRY AND PORK. Skinless white-meat poultry can serve as a good source of protein. However, higher-fat dark meat and poultry with skin-on are less healthful. Many pork products contain too much fat and sodium to belong in an anti-inflammatory diet, but very lean pork, such as pork tenderloin, can be enjoyed occasionally.

NATURAL SUGARS. We all deserve a treat, and nobody wants to feel deprived. When your sweet tooth does strike, the best sweets to choose, in moderation, are natural sugars such as honey, maple syrup, and molasses rather than refined sugar products. These offer some trace micronutrients, along with the sweet taste we crave.

Unique Bodies, Unique Reactions to Food

We also treat the "Big 8" food allergens (fish, shellfish, peanuts, tree nuts, wheat, soy, eggs, and dairy) as "Consider with Care" foods, to highlight them for those individuals who need to make substitutions. Food allergies are immune system responses in which the body mistakenly responds to proteins, in otherwise wholesome foods, as a threat. Food allergies can be life threatening, and those with food allergies know they must be vigilant to ensure they are not accidentally consuming foods that will stimulate a negative immune response.

Some people have sensitivities and intolerances to particular foods that are not technically allergies, as they do not involve the immune system. The research into this area is growing but still inconclusive; for many individuals, the best barometer for food tolerance comes from simply paying attention to how you feel after consuming that food. You know your own body best, so please modify the diet we present here to your needs. If you are uncertain about how well a particular food fits into your own dietary pattern, keep note of how you react when you eat that food, and consider consulting with a registered dietitian.

For those who can consume fish and shellfish, these are potent inflammation fighters. Deep-water fish offer unparalleled amounts of omega-3 fats in a form that is very easy for the body to use in fighting inflammation, so salmon and herring can be regular staples of your diet if you are not allergic.

Peanuts and tree nuts (walnuts, cashews, etc.) are anti-inflammatory powerhouses. If you're able to eat them, small portions of almonds or pecans provide the antioxidant vitamin E, healthy fats, and a bit of protein in addition to their rich, satisfying crunch.

Most people can consume nutritious ancient grains with no problems. If you have celiac disease or are intolerant or allergic to gluten, you'll want to avoid wheat berries and barley. Ancient grains may be avoided on strict elimination diets, which are not necessary for most people wanting to reduce inflammation. We also list the more processed whole-grain products under "Consider with Care." Whole-wheat bread is a step in the right direction from white bread, but it is still highly processed. Intact whole grains such as quinoa reign supreme for their anti-inflammatory power.

Soy is a major allergen but also a powerful inflammation fighter. Despite widespread myths, research shows that soy reduces inflammation and cancer risks for most people—great news if you enjoy popping steamed edamame in your mouth at your favorite sushi restaurant! Soy is a high-protein source of fiber, so unless you have an allergy, freely include edamame and tofu in your diet.

Eggs offer micronutrients such as choline and lutein, but they're another common allergen. While they do not appear to have specifically anti-inflammatory properties, they can serve as a good protein source in a healthy, balanced diet. If you can, consider including eggs as part of your overall dietary strategy.

Dairy is another major food allergen. Low- or non-fat dairy products, and those cultured to provide probiotics, like yogurt and kefir, should be considered with care. There is controversy over the benefits of including full-fat dairy in one's diet, but in relation to inflammation, the picture is clearer. Sources of saturated fat, like butter and cream, are best limited on an anti-inflammatory diet, so we don't use them here.

Anti-Inflammatory Food Lists

Foods in the "Enjoy" section can be eaten freely by most people. Challenge yourself to try them all! "Consider with Care" foods are nutritious for many people to consume as part of an otherwise balanced meal pattern. If you have a food allergy or other health consideration, choose one of the other options provided. The "Avoid" foods promote inflammation and can derail your efforts. Look for ways to swap those out for foods on the "Enjoy" list!

Benefits You'll See

Change can be hard—even positive change! As you begin this diet, you may find yourself challenged as you begin thinking about your meal choices in unfamiliar ways. That's a great reason to use the shopping lists and meal plans as we've presented them. This will take the guesswork and decision making out of the early stages of your transition to an anti-inflammatory lifestyle. Then you'll build confidence to begin testing out variations that work for you.

At first, you will notice that you are satisfied after each meal or snack, and that the energy you feel is more lasting throughout your day. You may find yourself getting hungry less often; this is because you're consuming more nutrient-dense foods. You may even see your skin clearing up as you remove highly processed foods and added sugars and replace them with more nourishing options that support health at the cellular level. Many people who shift to this eating style report gradual weight loss over time, which is also beneficial for reducing inflammation.

Less visible but equally important are the longer-term improvements you may notice in your health. If you happen to get a blood test from your doctor, you'll probably see the markers of inflammation, such as C-reactive protein (CRP) and interleukin 6 (IL-6), going down, and a more healthy lipid profile— higher HDL ("good") cholesterol and lower LDL ("bad") cholesterol—emerging over time. Your energy will likely be increasingly vibrant yet grounded and calm, and your body will be better able to fight off infection, whether that means just a little cold or a more significant threat. Your energy will increase, you will be better equipped to manage stress, and you'll just feel better—all qualities that can't be quantified in a lab test. Rather, you'll notice it when you bound out of bed in the morning, feeling great and ready to tackle the day—after a nourishing and satisfying anti-inflammatory breakfast, that is!

FOODS TO ENJOY

VEGETABLES (FRESH, FROZEN, OR CANNED WITHOUT ADDED SODIUM)

Alliums

Chives

Garlic*

Leeks

Onions*

Scallions

Shallots

Cruciferous Vegetables*

Arugula

Bok choy

Broccoli

Brussels sprouts

Cabbage

Cauliflower

Collard greens

Kale

Kohlrabi

Mizuna

Mustard greens

Radish greens

Romanesco broccoli/Roman cauliflower

Turnip greens

Dark Green Leafy Vegetables

Lettuces, especially romaine*

Spinach*

Swiss chard*

Root Vegetables

Beets

Carrots

Celery root/celeriac

Radishes

Rutabagas

Sweet potatoes

Turnips

Winter squash

Other Vegetables

Asparagus

Bell peppers

Corn

Fermented, probiotic vegetables*

Green beans

Mushrooms

FRUIT (FRESH, FROZEN, OR CANNED WITHOUT
ADDED SUGAR)

Apples

Apricots

Avocados

Bananas

Berries*

Citrus*

Cranberries

Figs

Grapes

Kiwi

Mangos

Melons

Pineapple*

Stone fruit

FATS AND OILS

Nut oils

Olive oil*

Seed oils

WHOLE AND ANCIENT GRAINS

Amaranth*

Brown rice

Buckwheat*

Millet*

Oatmeal*

Popcorn

Quinoa*

Teff*

SEEDS

Chia

Flaxseed*

Hemp

Mustard

Poppy

Pumpkin

Sesame

Sunflower

HERBS AND SPICES

Basil

Bay leaf

Cilantro

Cinnamon*

Clove

Dill

Ginger*

Mint

Nutmeg

Oregano*

Paprika

Parsley

Pepper

Rosemary*

Saffron*

Sage

Tarragon

Thyme

Turmeric*

PROTEINS

Beans*

Tempeh*

Tofu

OTHER

Unsweetened coffee

Unsweetened black or green tea*

Note: Asterisks indicate foods that are particularly beneficial anti-inflammatory superstars.

CONSIDER WITH CARE

FATS AND OILS

Coconut

Corn

Safflower

Sesame

Soy

Sunflower

WHOLE AND ANCIENT GRAINS

Barley

Emmer

Farro

Rye

Spelt

Wheat berries

Whole-grain breads, bulgur, couscous, pastas

NUTS AND SEEDS

Peanuts

Tree nuts* (e.g., almonds, cashews, macadamias, pistachios, walnuts*)

DAIRY

Fermented, probiotic dairy* (e.g., kefir, yogurt)

Low-fat and non-fat dairy products (e.g., cheese, milk)

PROTEINS

Eggs

Fish* (e.g., cod, flounder, halibut, mackerel, salmon,* sardines,* tuna)

Pork (very lean cuts, such as pork tenderloin)

Poultry (skinless white meat)

Shellfish (e.g., mussels, oysters, scallops)

Soy (e.g., edamame/soybeans, tofu, tempeh)

OTHER

Dark chocolate

Red wine

AVOID

FATS AND OILS

Butter

Lard

Margarine

GRAINS

All refined grains (e.g., white bread and rolls, white pasta, white rice)

Packaged, processed grain-based snacks and desserts (e.g., biscuits, cakes, cereals, cookies, crackers, muffins)

Pastries

OTHER

Bacon

Beef (especially high-fat cuts, beef charred on the grill, and corn-fed beef—typically any that is not grass-fed)

Full-fat dairy (e.g., butter, cheese, cream, half-and-half, ice cream)

High-fat foods (especially those with high saturated fats or trans fats)

High-sodium foods

Packaged and processed foods

Packaged, processed meat alternatives (e.g., "garden burgers," faux chicken)

Refined added sugars (brown sugar, confectioners' sugar, high-fructose corn syrup, white sugar)

Chapter 6: Weight Loss and the Importance of Calories

Obesity is one of these, especially if you have one of those "apple-shaped" body types where you are thicker around the middle. As previously noted, the visceral belly fat that hangs out among the organs of your abdomen does produce more of the markers in your blood stream that tell your physician that you are suffering from inflammation. The more of this "belly fat" that can be reduced, the better control you have over the reduction of those produced chemicals that aid in the development and flare ups of inflammation.

Lose Weight and Feel Great with the Anti-Inflammatory Diet

By slimming down, diminishing the amount of body fat you hold all together, you will begin to decrease the size of those visceral fat cells. The nice, added benefits include a weight loss that helps decrease or eliminate extra pressure on our joints and organs, in turn helping to alleviate some of the pain initially compounded by the inflammation.

One example that helps to explain this is the ratio of pounds to pressure on the knees. One extra pound of weight on your body exerts four extra pounds of pressure on your knees. It is how the body is built to distribute the weight. This means that by losing only ten pounds, you will reduce the amount of pressure on your knees by forty pounds!

Consider how it feels lifting forty pounds of groceries from the car (there are many who can't even do that much in one shot). Think about how you feel when you carry them into the house. The movement, the walking, etc. Adds that additional pressure to the joints of the knees, not to mention the arms, shoulders, and back. When they are put down, your body heaves a little sigh of relief. That extra weight pulling and pressing on our joints and muscles can hurt!

When you lose ten pounds, you are removing an extra forty pounds in just pain and pressure on the knees, let alone how it affects your other joints and muscles. Your body becomes more agreeable and maybe nags you just a little less. After all, pain is the body's way of telling you that something needs to change. It is protecting itself. You are coming to an agreement with your body that you will stop and reduce the pressure that you have been putting on it, while it, in turn, responds by agreeing to reduce the pain it has been causing with its nagging for you to take better care of it.

Let's take a look at a few other things that can help you have more agreeable communication with your body. Movement is one of these. If you are like most people, when you are in pain, or even feeling the general "ick" that comes with inflammation, the last thing you feel like is moving or doing anything that will draw your attention to the pain. And yet, what happens when you sit too long in one position and then have to get up and move anyway, for whatever reason? Your muscles and joints groan loudly in protest because they were quite comfortable with sitting still, pretending they didn't hurt in the first place. Your immediate reaction is usually one of not wanting to move because it hurts, and no one wants to hurt!

But we all do have to move at some point. When you start from a place of inaction—non-movement—your muscles and connective tissues for the joints stubbornly tighten up. It takes you a moment or more to get moving again, as you have to push past the tightness, which admittedly tends to hurt more at the beginning and then usually lessens as you keep going. By making movement a natural part of your day, you reduce the amount of stiffness that sets in, in turn reducing the amount of pain you feel when you do need to move.

Why does this happen? Besides the stiffening up and pain avoidance response, when muscles are not used, they start to weaken. When you don't continue to put weight on your bones, they lose density and weaken. The nervous system, which interacts with every part of your bodily functions, start to weaken their connection. Are you seeing a pattern here?

Healthy people who begin exercise and/or weight-lifting routines usually go through periods of muscle strain and bone ache as they begin to push their bodies to do more than they previously had. But as they push through and continue, their muscles and organs start to build up to work better together. Even the heart gets healthier as it works to keep up with the extra blood needed to be pumped to feed the level of activity that is now occurring. The capacity of the lungs increases as the demand for oxygen in the blood and to the organs increases to compensate for the healthier, growing masses of muscle and organs working together more efficiently and harmoniously. When you go to move, the body

is better prepared and doesn't give you the pain response in a protective warning.

Wouldn't it be nice to move without the anticipation of your body's bombardment of pain and protest? Of course! Unfortunately, not everyone, especially those suffering from inflammation or other reasons for long periods of inactivity, can just jump right into a strenuous regime of exercise and muscle building. If they were, they probably wouldn't be so desperately trying to find some way to reduce the pain and stress in their lives and bodies. In addition, some forms of strenuous exercise, when not properly done, can actually cause more damage to the body, and potentially increase inflammation with that damage.

Chapter 7: Planning a proper diet plan

Eat more plants. Explore and enjoy the wide range of fruits and vegetables that provide fiber, antioxidants, and other nutrients to support optimal health. These low-calorie foods combat cellular damage, promote digestion, and help maintain a healthy weight range, which keeps inflammation in check as well.

Discover whole and ancient grains. Ancient grains are those that predate modern varieties created through selective breeding and hybridization—think oats, barley, chia, sorghum, quinoa, bulgur, and the like. These and whole grains retain fiber, antioxidants, and other nutrients that promote a healthy immune response. If whole grains are new to you, try mixing them 50/50 with your usual choice to begin dining the anti-inflammatory way, such as white rice with brown rice, quinoa with couscous, or whole-wheat bread crumbs with white.

Choose healthy fats. Plant-based options like olive oil contain unsaturated fats that support immunity. These are preferable to proinflammatory trans fats and saturated fats from animal products, like butter and bacon. Look for omega-3 fats, such as fish and walnuts, to directly reduce inflammation.

Enjoy nuts and seeds. These little bites provide healthy fats and protein, as well as valuable micronutrients and fiber. Plus, their flavor and crunch enhance any meal or snack.

Add flavor with herbs and spices. Turmeric, ginger, and garlic are anti-inflammatory powerhouses. Have fun exploring these and countless other options for their deep flavors and unique benefits.

Support your microbiome. High-fiber foods like beans and whole grains provide nourishment for your beneficial gut bacteria to thrive. Fermented foods such as yogurt, kimchi, and pickles keep the "communities" of bacteria in your digestive system balanced to help fight inflammation and disease.

Consume power beverages. Coffee and unsweetened black or green tea offer antioxidant compounds that promote resilience against cell damage. Enjoy red wine on occasion, if you like, to maximize anti-inflammatory benefits. Plain water is always a great choice for keeping your body hydrated and energized—vary the flavor and benefits by tossing in some cut fruit or herbs.

Eat fewer processed foods. Highly processed foods are often high in added sugars, refined grains, sodium, and detrimental fats. These types of foods are proinflammatory and also increase one's risk for weight gain and other diseases. If you haven't yet, become a label reader to increase your awareness of what's in these foods—it may surprise and inspire you to run toward the whole foods sections of the store.

Consume less meat. When you want meat, choose and prepare it carefully. Many meats have undesirable amounts of unhealthy fats, and some are pumped full of sodium during processing. Use cooking methods that do not blacken the meat, such as grilling, as the blackened parts that occur have compounds that can contribute to inflammation.

Relax! Stress is a significant contributor to inflammation and disease—in fact, chronic elevation of the stress hormone cortisol leads to ongoing negative impacts on health. Get more sleep, boost your physical activity, and try new activities such as mindfulness meditation—these all help manage stress and keep inflammation down.

Chapter 8: Balancing your Calorie intake

With obesity, for example, a series of causes and effects interact with each other in a downward spiral of declining health. Chronic, low-grade inflammation results directly from consumption of excess calories and obesity. As fat tissue increases, it releases chemicals, hormones, and immune cells that can disrupt normal body function. Proinflammatory cytokines are also released, leading to higher levels of inflammation throughout the body. As the internal system becomes more imbalanced, the risk of developing chronic disorders such as cardiovascular disease, hypertension, type 2 diabetes, and various cancers increases. Many of these conditions increase inflammation themselves. It can become quite complicated when so many of the body's systems are poorly regulated and caught in a feedback loop of actively causing inflammation and damage to other systems.

But there's good news! Consuming anti-inflammatory foods can help straighten out the whole situation, whatever it may be rooted in. An anti-inflammatory diet can support healing if inflammation already exists, and it will provide a foundation for resilience in the future. Shift your focus to this kind of nourishing, balanced, and tasty diet and you'll see a difference in no time, as this diet will restore the energy and sense of well-being you deserve.

Principles of the Anti-Inflammatory Diet

Experts agree that a diet consisting of a wide range of plant-based foods, accompanied by moderate amounts of whole grains, lean proteins, and healthful fats, is the type of eating pattern that will reduce inflammation and ensure a robust immune system. We are constantly learning more about the negative effects of heavily processed, packaged foods, which are often high in inflammation-promoting sodium, added sugars, refined grains, and detrimental fats. Conversely, this book emphasizes fresh, whole foods that are prepared using healthy cooking techniques. Vibrant herbs and spices are not just good for punching up flavor—you'll learn how each brings its own health-supportive qualities to your meals. Prebiotic and probiotic foods support your microbiome—that's the name for the beneficial gut bacteria in your digestive system. These bacteria are linked to a thriving immune system. And you can wash it all down with powerful inflammation-fighting beverages such as unsweetened tea and coffee, water infused with herbs or fruit, and the occasional glass of red wine, if you choose to partake.

We present recipes inspired by the many traditional cuisines around the world that promote a vigorous immune response. Traditional Japanese diets, for instance, are low in fat and full of nutrient-rich vegetables and seafood, but contain very little sugar or refined flour. A modified paleo approach is also explored here, including generous portions of vegetables and hearty protein dishes prepared from the healthiest meats. The Mediterranean eating pattern is well studied for its anti-inflammatory, health-promoting qualities, and many people find its familiar flavors satisfying and appealing. It is based on abundant fruits and vegetables, along with whole grains, legumes, and nuts. Fish, red wine, and olive oil are incorporated regularly in Mediterranean cooking, while red meat, added sugars, and high-fat dairy are limited. We are inspired by this delicious style of eating, so you'll see a lot of recipes here that reflect the Mediterranean approach. But we also recognize that the only anti-inflammatory diet that will work for you is the one you find satisfying and delicious. So after you master the basics, use these principles to figure out which styles you enjoy best and fine-tune your own anti-inflammatory lifestyle path!

Chapter 9: Breakfast Recipes

Zucchini and Sprout Breakfast Mix

Preparation time: 10 minutes

Cooking time: 0 minutes

Servings: 4

Ingredients:

2 zucchinis, spiralized

2 cups bean sprouts

4 green onions, chopped

1 red bell pepper, chopped

Juice of 1 lime

1 tablespoon olive oil

½ cup chopped cilantro

¾ cup almonds chopped

A pinch of salt and black pepper

Directions:

In a salad bowl, toss together the zucchinis with the bean sprouts, green onions, bell pepper, cilantro, almonds, salt, pepper, limejuice and oil. Serve for breakfast.

Nutrition Values: calories 140, fat 4, fiber 2, carbs 7, protein 8

Tomato and Olive Salad

Preparation time: 10 minutes

Cooking time: 0 minutes

Servings: 4

Ingredients:

2 cups baby spinach, torn

2 cups cherry tomatoes, halved

4 tablespoons chopped red onion

1 cup chopped cucumber

1 cup kalamata olives, pitted and sliced

1 tablespoon chopped dill

3 tablespoons lemon juice

A pinch of salt and black pepper

2 tablespoons olive oil

Directions:

In a salad bowl, toss the spinach with the tomatoes, onion, cucumber, olives, dill, lemon juice, salt, pepper and oil. Serve for breakfast.

Enjoy!

Nutrition Values: calories 171, fat 2, fiber 5, carbs 11, protein 5

Blueberry and Cashew Mix

Preparation time: 10 minutes

Cooking time: 12 minutes

Servings: 2

Ingredients:

2 bananas, peeled and sliced

¼ cup cashews

¼ cup blueberries

1 tablespoon almond butter

1/3 cup coconut flakes, unsweetened

1 cup coconut milk, unsweetened

Directions:

In a small pot, mix the berries with the coconut flakes, milk, cashews, almond butter and bananas. Mix together and bring to a simmer over medium heat. Cook for 12 minutes, divide into bowls and serve for breakfast.

Enjoy!

Nutrition Values: calories 370, fat 23, fiber 6, carbs 40, protein 8

Easy Almond Zucchini Bowl

Preparation time: 10 minutes

Cooking time: 15 minutes

Servings: 2

Ingredients:

1 cup egg whites, whisked

1½ tablespoons ground flaxseed

1 cup almond milk, unsweetened

1 banana, peeled and mashed

1 small zucchini, grated

½ teaspoon ground cinnamon

Directions:

In a small pan, combine the milk with the egg whites, flaxseed, banana, zucchini and cinnamon powder. Bring to a simmer, mixing constantly, over medium heat. Cook for 15 minutes, divide into bowls and serve for breakfast.

Enjoy!

Nutrition Values: calories 201, fat 6, fiber 9, carbs 14, protein 6

Sweet Potato Hash

Preparation time: 10 minutes

Cooking time: 15 minutes

Servings: 4

Ingredients:

1 sweet potato, peeled and cubed

1 celery root, peeled and cubed

1 cup coconut milk

2 tablespoons olive oil

1 small yellow onion, chopped

1 teaspoon smoked paprika

4 garlic cloves, minced

2 tablespoons parsley, chopped

A pinch of salt and black pepper

Directions:

Heat up a pan with the oil over medium-high heat. Add the celery root and the sweet potato, toss and cook for 5 minutes. Add the onion, garlic, salt, pepper, parsley and paprika then toss and cook for 8 minutes more. Add the coconut milk, mix and cook for 1-2 minutes. Divide everything into bowls and serve for breakfast.

Enjoy!

Nutrition Values: calories 188, fat 2, fiber 8, carbs 10, protein 4

Zucchini Breakfast Salad

Preparation time: 10 minutes

Cooking time: 0 minutes

Servings: 4

Ingredients:

2 zucchinis, spiralized

1 cup beets, baked, peeled and grated

½ bunch kale, chopped

2 tablespoons olive oil

For the tahini sauce:

1 tablespoon maple syrup

Juice of 1 lime

¼ inch fresh ginger, grated

1/3 cup sesame seed paste

Directions:

In a salad bowl, mix the zucchinis with the beets, kale and oil. In another small bowl, whisk the maple syrup with lime juice, ginger and sesame paste. Pour the dressing over the salad, toss and serve it for breakfast.

Enjoy!

Nutrition Values: calories 183, fat 3, fiber 2, carbs 7, protein 9

Quinoa and Spinach Breakfast Salad

Preparation time: 10 minutes

Cooking time: 0 minutes

Servings: 2

Ingredients:

16 ounces quinoa, cooked

1 handful raisins

1 handful baby spinach leaves

1 tablespoon maple syrup

½ tablespoon lemon juice

4 tablespoons olive oil

1 teaspoon ground cumin

A pinch of sea salt and black pepper

½ teaspoon chili flakes

Directions:

In a bowl, mix the quinoa with the spinach, raisins, cumin, salt and pepper and toss. Add the maple syrup, lemon juice, oil and chili flakes and toss then serve for breakfast.

Enjoy!

Nutrition Values: calories 170, fat 3, fiber 6, carbs 8, protein 5

Carrots Breakfast Mix

Preparation time: 10 minutes

Cooking time: 0 minutes

Servings: 4

Ingredients:

1½ tablespoon maple syrup

1 teaspoon olive oil

1 tablespoon chopped walnuts

1 onion, chopped

4 cups shredded carrots

1 tablespoon curry powder

¼ teaspoon ground turmeric

Black pepper to the taste

2 tablespoons sesame seed paste

¼ cup lemon juice

½ cup chopped parsley

Directions:

In a salad bowl, mix together the onion with the carrots, turmeric, curry powder, black pepper, lemon juice and parsley. Add the maple syrup, oil, walnuts and sesame seed paste. toss well and serve for breakfast.

Enjoy!

Nutrition Values: calories 150, fat 3, fiber 2, carbs 6, protein 8

Avocado Omelet

Preparation time: 10 minutes

Cooking time: 10 minutes

Servings: 2

Ingredients:

4 eggs, whisked

2 avocados, pitted, peeled and cubed

A pinch of salt and black pepper

Juice of ½ lemon

1 tablespoon chopped parsley

1 tablespoon olive oil

Directions:

In a bowl, mix the eggs with the avocados, salt, pepper, lemon juice and parsley. Heat up a pan with the oil over medium-high heat then add the avocado and egg mix, spread into the pan and cook for 4 minutes on each side. Divide between plates and serve for breakfast.

Enjoy!

Nutrition Values: calories 201, fat 2, fiber 5, carbs 11, protein 5

Italian Breakfast Salad

Preparation time: 10 minutes

Cooking time: 0 minutes

Servings: 4

Ingredients:

1 handful kalamata olives, pitted and sliced

1 cup cherry tomatoes, halved

1½ cucumbers, sliced

1 red onion, chopped

2 tablespoons chopped oregano

1 tablespoon chopped mint

For the salad dressing:

2 tablespoons balsamic vinegar

¼ cup olive oil

1 garlic clove, minced

2 teaspoons dried Italian herbs

A pinch of salt and black pepper

Directions:

In a salad bowl, toss together the olives with the tomatoes, cucumbers, onion, mint and oregano. In a smaller bowl, whisk the vinegar with the oil, garlic, Italian herbs, salt and pepper. Pour the dressing over the salad, toss and serve for breakfast.

Enjoy!

Nutrition Values: calories 191, fat 10, fiber 3, carbs 13, protein 1

Broccoli and Squash Mix

Preparation time: 10 minutes

Cooking time: 15 minutes

Servings: 4

Ingredients:

4 cups spaghetti squash, peeled, cooked and flesh scrapped out

1½ cups broccoli florets

1 tablespoon olive oil

1 cup coconut milk, unsweetened

1 egg, whisked

1 teaspoon garlic powder

A pinch of salt and black pepper

Directions:

Heat up a pan with the oil over medium-high heat, add the spaghetti squash and the broccoli. Stir and cook for 5-6 minutes. Add the garlic powder, salt, pepper, garlic powder and the egg. Stir and cook for 5 minutes more. Add the coconut milk, mix and cook for about 5 minutes more then divide into bowls and serve for breakfast.

Enjoy!

Nutrition Values: calories 207, fat 5, fiber 8, carbs 14, protein 7

Greens and Berries Mix

Preparation time: 10 minutes

Cooking time: 0 minutes

Servings: 2

Ingredients:

½ cup spinach, torn

½ cup kale, torn

1 cup strawberries, halved

1 cup blueberries

1 banana, peeled and chopped

6 mint leaves, chopped

Directions:

In a bowl, mix the spinach with the kale, strawberries, blueberries, banana and mint. Serve for breakfast.

Enjoy!

Nutrition Values: calories 198, fat 4, fiber 2, carbs 8, protein 6

Veggie and Eggs

Preparation time: 10 minutes

Cooking time: 15 minutes

Servings: 6

Ingredients:

1 red bell pepper, chopped

4 cherry tomatoes, chopped

3 spring onions, chopped

A handful kale, torn

1 tablespoon olive oil

6 eggs

A pinch of salt and black pepper

A pinch of curry powder

Directions:

Heat up a pan with the oil over medium-high heat, add the onions, stir and cook for 1-2 minutes. Add the bell pepper, the tomatoes, the kale, salt, pepper and the curry powder, stir and cook for 4-5 minutes. Crack the eggs into the pan and mix well. Cook until the eggs are done, divide between plates and serve for breakfast.

Enjoy!

Nutrition Values: calories 106, fat 8, fiber 1, carbs 4, protein 7

Coconut Pear Bowl

Preparation time: 10 minutes

Cooking time: 15 minutes

Servings: 4

Ingredients:

2 cups coconut milk, unsweetened

1/3 cup coconut flakes, unsweetened

½ teaspoon vanilla extract

3 pears, peeled, cored and cubed

1. **Directions:**

Put the milk in a small pot, add the coconut, vanilla and pears. Stir and bring to a simmer over medium heat, cook for 15 minutes, divide into bowls and serve.

Enjoy!

Nutrition Values: calories 172, fat 5, fiber 7, carbs 8, protein 4

Breakfast Corn Salad

Preparation time: 10 minutes

Cooking time: 0 minutes

Servings: 4

Ingredients:

2 avocados, pitted, peeled and cubed

1-pint mixed cherry tomatoes, halved

2 cups fresh corn kernels

1 red onion, chopped

For the salad dressing:

2 tablespoons olive oil

1 tablespoon lime juice

½ teaspoon grated lime zest

A pinch of salt and black pepper

¼ cup chopped cilantro

Directions:

In a salad bowl, mix the avocados with the tomatoes, corn and onion. Add the oil, lime juice, lime zest, salt, pepper and the cilantro, toss and serve for breakfast.

Nutrition Values: calories 140, fat 3, fiber 2, carbs 6, protein 9

Simple Basil Tomato Mix

Preparation time: 10 minutes

Cooking time: 0 minutes

Servings: 6

Ingredients:

½ cup extra-virgin olive oil

1 cucumber, chopped

2 pints colored cherry tomatoes, halved

Salt and black pepper to the taste

1 red onion, chopped

3 tablespoons red vinegar

1 garlic clove, minced

1 bunch basil, roughly chopped

Directions:

In a salad bowl, toss together the cucumber with the tomatoes, onion, salt, pepper, oil, vinegar, basil and garlic. Serve for breakfast.

Enjoy!

Nutrition Values: calories 100, fat 1, fiber 2, carbs 2, protein 6

Cucumber and Avocado Salad

Preparation time: 10 minutes

Cooking time: 0 minutes

Servings: 4

Ingredients:

1 pound cucumbers, chopped

2 avocados, pitted and chopped

1 small red onion, thinly sliced

2 tablespoons olive oil

2 tablespoons lemon juice

¼ cup chopped parsley

A pinch of salt and black pepper

Directions:

In a salad bowl, mix together the cucumbers with the avocados, onion, oil, lemon juice, parsley, salt and pepper. Serve for breakfast.

Enjoy!

Nutrition Values: calories 120, fat 2, fiber 2, carbs 3, protein 4

Watermelon Salad

Preparation time: 10 minutes

Cooking time: 0 minutes

Servings: 2

Ingredients:

½ teaspoon agave nectar

2 tablespoons lemon juice

1 tablespoon extra-virgin olive oil

1 jalapeno, seeded and chopped

12 ounces watermelon, chopped

1 red onion, thinly sliced

½ cup chopped basil leaves

2 cups baby arugula

Directions:

In a bowl, toss together the watermelon with the jalapeno, onion, basil, arugula, oil, agave nectar, lemon juice and oil. Serve for breakfast.

Nutrition Values: calories 128, fat 8, fiber 2, carbs 16, protein 2

Coconut Porridge

Preparation time: 10 minutes

Cooking time: 15 minutes

Servings: 2

Ingredients:

2 cups coconut milk, unsweetened

3 tablespoons almond flour

½ cup coconut flakes, unsweetened

2 tablespoons ground flax meal

1 teaspoon vanilla extract

2 teaspoons ground cinnamon

Directions:

In a small pot, mix the coconut milk with the almond flour, coconut flakes, flax meal, vanilla and cinnamon. Stir and bring to a simmer over medium heat for 15 minutes. Divide into bowls and serve for breakfast.

Enjoy!

Nutrition Values: calories 287, fat 5, fiber 7, carbs 13, protein 5

Blackberry and Strawberry Salad

Preparation time: 5 minutes

Cooking time: 0 minutes

Servings: 1

Ingredients:

¼ cup sliced almonds

¼ cup blackberries

¼ cup strawberries, halved

1 banana, peeled and sliced

A pinch of ground cinnamon

Directions:

In a bowl, mix the blackberries with strawberries, cinnamon, banana and almonds. Serve for breakfast.

Enjoy!

Nutrition Values: calories 90, fat 3, fiber 1, carbs 0, protein 5

Breakfast Kale Frittata

Preparation time: 10 minutes

Cooking time: 30 minutes

Servings: 4

Ingredients:

6 kale stalks, chopped

1 small sweet onion, chopped

1 small broccoli head, florets separated

2 garlic cloves, minced

Salt and black pepper to the taste

4 eggs

1 tablespoon olive oil

Directions:

Heat up a pan with the oil over medium-high heat, add the onion, stir and cook for 4-5 minutes. Add the garlic, broccoli and kale, toss and cook for 5 minutes more. Add the eggs, salt and pepper and mix. Place in the oven and bake at 380 degrees F for 20 minutes. Slice and serve for breakfast.

Enjoy!

Nutrition Values: calories 214, fat 7, fiber 2, carbs 12, protein 8

Cranberry Granola Bars

Preparation time: 2 hours

Cooking time: 0 minutes

Servings: 4

Ingredients:

2 cups walnuts, toasted

1 cup dates, pitted

3 tablespoons water

¾ cup cranberries, dried, no added sugar

2 cups desiccated coconut, unsweetened

Directions:

In your food processor, mix dates with coconut, cranberries, water and walnuts. Pulse really well then spread the mix into a lined baking dish. Press well into the dish and keep in the fridge for 2 hours then cut into bars and serve.

Enjoy!

Nutrition Values: calories 476, fat 40, fiber 9, carbs 33, protein 6

Spinach and Berry Smoothie

Preparation time: 10 minutes

Cooking time: 0 minutes

Servings: 2

Ingredients:

1 cup blackberries

1 avocado, pitted, peeled and chopped

1 banana, peeled and roughly chopped

1 cup baby spinach

1 tablespoon hemp seeds

1 cup water

½ cup almond milk, unsweetened

Directions:

In your blender, mix the berries with the avocado, banana, spinach, hemp seeds, water and almond milk. Pulse well, divide into 2 glasses and serve for breakfast.

Enjoy!

Nutrition Values: calories 160, fat 3, fiber 4, carbs 6, protein 3

Chapter 10: Lunch Recipes

Tasty Grilled Asparagus

Preparation time: 10 minutes

Cooking time: 6 minutes

Servings: 4

Ingredients:

2 pounds asparagus, trimmed

2 tablespoons organic olive oil

A pinch of salt and black pepper

Directions:

In a bowl, combine the asparagus with salt, pepper and oil and toss well.

Place the asparagus on preheated grill over medium-high heat, cook for 3 minutes with them, divide between plates and serve as being a side dish.

Enjoy!

Nutrition Values: calories 172, fat 4, fiber 7, carbs 14, protein 8

Easy Roasted Carrots

Preparation time: ten mins

Cooking time: 30 minutes

Servings: 4

Ingredients:

2 pounds carrots, quartered

A pinch of black pepper

3 tablespoons olive oil

2 tablespoons parsley, chopped

Directions:

Arrange the carrots with a lined baking sheet, add black pepper and oil, toss, introduce inside the oven and cook at 400 degrees F to get a half-hour.

Add parsley, toss, divide between plates and serve as a side dish.

Enjoy!

Nutrition Values: calories 177, fat 3, fiber 6, carbs 14, protein 6

Oven Roasted Asparagus

Preparation time: 10 mins

Cooking time: 25 minutes

Servings: 4

Ingredients:

2 pounds asparagus spears, trimmed

3 tablespoons essential organic olive oil

A pinch of black pepper

2 teaspoons sweet paprika

1 teaspoon sesame seeds

Directions:

Arrange the asparagus on the lined baking sheet, add oil, black pepper and paprika, toss, introduce inside oven and bake at 400 degrees F for 25 minutes.

Divide the asparagus between plates, sprinkle sesame seeds ahead and serve as being a side dish.

Enjoy!

Nutrition Values: calories 190, fat 4, fiber 8, carbs 11, protein 5

Squash Side Salad

Preparation time: 10 minutes

Cooking time: a half-hour

Servings: 6

Ingredients:

1 cup orange juice

3 tablespoons coconut sugar

1 and ½ tablespoons mustard

1 tablespoon ginger, grated

1 and ½ pounds butternut squash, peeled and roughly cubed

Cooking spray

A pinch of black pepper

1/3 cup extra virgin olive oil

6 cups salad greens

1 radicchio, sliced

½ cup pistachios, roasted

Directions:

In a bowl, combine the orange juice with all the sugar, mustard, ginger, black pepper and squash, toss well, spread on a lined baking sheet, spray everything with oil, introduce inside oven and bake at 400 degrees F for thirty minutes.

In a salad bowl, combine the squash with salad greens, radicchio, pistachios and oil, toss well, divide between plates and serve like a side dish.

Enjoy!

Nutrition Values: calories 275, fat 3, fiber 4, carbs 16, protein 6

Colored Iceberg Salad

Preparation time: ten mins

Cooking time: 0 minutes

Servings: 4

Ingredients:

1 iceberg lettuce head, leaves torn

6 bacon slices, cooked and halved

2 green onions, sliced

3 carrots, shredded

6 radishes, sliced

¼ cup red vinegar

¼ cup essential olive oil

3 garlic cloves, minced

A pinch of black pepper

Directions:

In a substantial salad bowl, combine the lettuce leaves with the bacon, green onions, carrots, radishes, vinegar, oil, garlic and black pepper, toss, divide between plates and serve being a side dish.

Enjoy!

Nutrition Values: calories 235, fat 4, fiber 4, carbs 10, protein 6

Fennel Side Salad

Preparation time: ten mins

Cooking time: 0 minutes

Servings: 4

Ingredients:

2 fennel bulbs, trimmed and shaved

1 and ¼ cups zucchini, sliced

2/3 cup dill, chopped

¼ cup freshly squeezed fresh lemon juice

¼ cup essential olive oil

6 cups arugula

½ cups walnuts, chopped

1/3 cup low-fat feta cheese, crumbled

Directions:

In a substantial bowl, combine the fennel while using zucchini, dill, fresh freshly squeezed lemon juice, arugula, oil, walnuts and cheese, toss, divide between plates and serve as a side dish.

Enjoy!

Nutrition Values: calories 188, fat 4, fiber 5, carbs 14, protein 6

Corn Mix

Preparation time: ten minutes

Cooking time: 0 minutes

Servings: 4

Ingredients:

½ cup cider vinegar

¼ cup coconut sugar

A pinch of black pepper

4 cups corn

½ cup red onion, chopped

½ cup cucumber, sliced

½ cup red bell pepper, chopped

½ cup cherry tomatoes, halved

3 tablespoons parsley, chopped

1 tablespoon basil, chopped

1 tablespoon jalapeno, chopped

2 cups baby arugula leaves

Directions:

In a big bowl, combine the corn with onion, cucumber, bell pepper, cherry tomatoes, parsley, basil, jalapeno and arugula and toss.

Add vinegar, sugar and black pepper, toss well, divide between plates and serve just like a side dish.

Enjoy!

Nutrition Values: calories 100, fat 2, fiber 3, carbs 14, protein 4

Persimmon Side Salad

Preparation time: ten mins

Cooking time: 0 minutes

Servings: 4

Ingredients:

Seeds from 1 pomegranate

2 persimmons, cored and sliced

5 cups baby arugula

6 tablespoons green onions, chopped

4 navel oranges, peeled and cut into segments

¼ cup apple cider vinegar

1/3 cup essential olive oil

3 tablespoons pine nuts

1 and ½ teaspoons orange zest, grated

2 tablespoons orange juice

1 tablespoon coconut sugar

½ shallot, chopped

A pinch of cinnamon powder

Directions:

In a salad bowl, combine the pomegranate seeds with persimmons, arugula, green onions and oranges and toss.

In another bowl, combine the vinegar with all the oil, pine nuts, orange zest, orange juice, sugar, shallot and cinnamon, whisk well, add to the salad, toss and serve like a side dish.

Enjoy!

Nutrition Values: calories 188, fat 4, fiber 4, carbs 14, protein 4

Roast green beans with cranberries

Preparation Time: 30 minutes

Servings: 4

Ingredients:

Halved green beans- 2 Ib.

Dried cranberries- ¼ cup

Chopped almonds -¼ cup

Olive oil- 3 tbsp.

Salt

Black pepper

Directions:

Arrange the green beans on a baking sheet and sprinkle oil, salt, and pepper on it.

Mix and roast in the oven for 15 minutes at 425°F.

Stir in the almonds and cranberries and cook for 5 minutes.

Serve.

Nutrition Values:

Calories 181, carbs 10, protein 6, fiber 5, fats 3

Roasted cheesy mushrooms

Preparation Time: 25 minutes

Servings: 4

Ingredients:

Sliced cremini mushrooms- 1½ Ib.

Grated zest of 1 lemon

Grated parmesan - ¼ cup

Dried thyme- 2 tsp.

Minced garlic cloves- 3

Lemon juice- ¼ cup

Olive oil- 3 tbsp.

Salt

Black pepper

Directions:

Coat the baking dish with oil and mix mushrooms with zest, juice, Parmesan, thyme, salt, pepper, and garlic.

Bake in the oven for 15 minutes at 375°F.

Serve.

Nutrition Values:

Calories 199, carbs 12, protein 7, fiber 7, fats 2

Herbed Pork

Preparation time: 10 mins

Cooking time: 60 minutes and 10 minutes

Servings: 6

Ingredients:

2 and ½ pounds pork loin boneless, trimmed and cubed

¾ cup low-sodium chicken stock

2 tablespoons extra virgin extra virgin olive oil

½ tablespoon sweet paprika

2 and ¼ teaspoon sage, dried

½ tablespoon garlic powder

¼ teaspoon rosemary, dried

¼ teaspoon marjoram, dried

1 teaspoon basil, dried

1 teaspoon oregano, dried black pepper

Directions:

In a bowl, mix oil with stock, paprika, garlic powder, sage, rosemary, thyme, marjoram, oregano and pepper for the taste and whisk well.

Heat up a pan over medium-high heat, add the pork and brown it for 5 minutes on either sides.

Add the herbed mix, toss well, cook over medium heat for an hour, divide between plates and serve employing a side salad.

Enjoy!

Nutrition Values: calories 310, fat 4, fiber 6, carbs 12, protein 14

Garlic Pork Shoulder

Preparation time: 10 mins

Cooking time: 4 hours and thirty minutes

Servings: 6

Ingredients:

3 tablespoons garlic, minced

3 tablespoons extra virgin essential olive oil

4 pounds pork shoulder

2 teaspoons sweet paprika

Black pepper for the taste

Directions:

In a bowl, mix extra virgin extra virgin olive oil with paprika, black pepper and oil and whisk well.

Brush pork shoulder with this mix, arrange inside a baking dish and introduce inside oven at 425 degrees for twenty or so minutes.

Reduce heat to 325 degrees F and bake for 4 hours.

Slice the meat, divide it between plates and serve having a side salad.

Enjoy!

Nutrition Values: calories 321, fat 6, fiber 4, carbs 12, protein 18

Pork and Creamy Veggie Sauce

Preparation time: 10 mins

Cooking time: one hour and twenty approximately minutes

Servings: 4

Ingredients:

2 pounds pork roast

1 cup low-sodium veggie stock

2 carrots, chopped

1 leek, chopped

1 celery stalk, chopped

1 teaspoon black peppercorns

2 yellow onions, cut into quarters

1 tablespoon chives, chopped

1 tablespoon parsley, chopped

2 cups nonfat yogurt

1 cup coconut cream

1 teaspoon mustard

Black pepper towards the taste

Directions:

Put the roast in a baking dish, add carrots, leek, celery, peppercorns, onions, stock and black pepper, cover, introduce inside oven and bake at 400 degrees F for sixty minutes and 10 minutes

Transfer the roast using a platter and all sorts of the veggies mix with a pan.

Heat this mix over medium heat, add yogurt, cream and mustard, toss, cook for ten mins, drizzle inside the roast and serve.

Enjoy!

Nutrition Values: calories 263, fat 4, fiber 2, carbs 12, protein 22

Ground Pork Pan

Preparation Time: 10 mins

Cooking time: 20 mins

Servings: 4

Ingredients:

Zest of merely one lemon, grated

Juice of a single lemon

2 garlic cloves, minced

1 tablespoon organic olive oil

1 pound pork meat, ground

Black pepper on the taste

1-pint cherry tomatoes, chopped

1 small red onion, chopped

½ cup low-sodium veggie stock,

2 tablespoons low-sodium tomato paste

1 tablespoon basil, chopped

Directions:

Heat up a pan with all the oil over medium heat, add garlic and onion, stir and cook for 5 minutes.

Add pork, black pepper, tomatoes, stock, freshly squeezed freshly squeezed lemon juice, lemon zest and tomato paste, toss and cook for quarter-hour.

Add basil, toss, divide between plates and serve.

Enjoy!

Nutrition Values: calories 286, fat 8, fiber 7, carbs 14, protein 17

Tarragon Pork Steak

Preparation time: 10 minutes

Cooking time: 22 minutes

Servings: 4

Ingredients:

4 medium pork steaks

Black pepper towards the taste

1 tablespoon extra virgin olive oil

8 cherry tomatoes, halved

A handful tarragon, chopped

Directions:

Heat up a pan while using the oil over medium-high heat, add steaks, season with black pepper, cook them for 6 minutes on each side and divide between plates.

Heat the same pan over medium heat, add the tomatoes along with the tarragon, cook for ten minutes, divide next around the pork and serve.

Enjoy!

Nutrition Values: calories 263, fat 4, fiber 6, carbs 12, protein 16

Pork Meatballs

Preparation time: ten minutes

Cooking time: 10 mins

Servings: 4

Ingredients:

1 pound pork, ground

1/3 cup cilantro, chopped

1 cup red onion, chopped

4 garlic cloves, minced

1 tablespoon ginger, grated

1 Thai chili, chopped

2 tablespoons extra virgin olive oil

Directions:

In a bowl, combine the meat with cilantro, onion, garlic, ginger and chili, stir well and shape medium meatballs out of this mix.

Heat up a pan while using oil over medium-high heat, add the meatballs, cook them for 5 minutes on either side, divide them between plates and serve with a side salad.

Enjoy!

Nutrition Values: calories 220, fat 4, fiber 2, carbs 8, protein 14

Nutmeg Meatballs Curry

Preparation Time: 40 minutes

Servings: 3

Ingredients:

Pork meat, ground- 2/3 lbs.

Egg -½

Parsley, chopped-1 tbsp

Coconut flour-2 tbsp

Garlic clove, minced-1

Salt and black pepper - to taste

Veggie stock -¼ cup

Tomato passata-½ cup

Nutmeg, ground -¼ tsp

Sweet paprika -¼ tsp

Olive oil-1 tbsp

Carrot, chopped -1

Directions:

Thoroughly mix the meat with egg, parsley, salt, pepper, garlic, nutmeg, and paprika in a suitable bowl.

Mix well and make small meatballs out of this mixture.

Dredge these balls through dry flour or dust the balls with flour.

Place a pot with oil over medium-high heat.

Add dusted meatballs in the pot and sear them for 4 minutes per side.

Toss in tomato passata, carrots, and stock.

Cover this mixture and let it simmer for 20 minutes.

Serve right away.

Devour.

Nutrition Values:

Calories: 281, Fat: 8, Fiber: 6, Carbs: 10, Protein: 15

Pan seared sausage and kale

Preparation Time: 35 minutes

Servings: 4

Ingredients:

Chopped kale- 5 Ib.

Italian pork sausage: sliced- 1½ Ib.

Minced garlic- 1 tsp.

Water- 1 cup

Onion: chopped- 1 cup

Red bell pepper: seeded and chopped ½ cup

Red chili pepper: chopped ½ cup

Black pepper

Salt

Directions:

Put a pan on medium heat and add the sausage to brown for 10 minutes.

Mix in onions and town for 3-4 minutes.

Add in the garlic and bell pepper and cook for 1 minute.

Mix in the chili, kale, water, pepper and salt and let cook for 10 minutes.

Serve

Nutrition Values:

Calories- 872, carbs- 61, protein- 54, fiber- 3, fats- 43

Pan-Fried Chorizo Mix

Preparation Time: 35 minutes

Servings: 4

Ingredients:

Chopped tomato, 1

Olive oil, 1 tbsp.

Sugar-free chorizo sausages, 2

Chopped zucchini, 1

Chopped red bell pepper, 1

Minced garlic cloves, 2

Black pepper

Chicken stock, 2 cup.

Chopped parsley, 2 tbsps.

Lemon juice, 1 tbsp.

Salt

Chopped yellow onion, 1

Directions:

Set the pan on fire to fry the chorizo and onion for 3 minutes over medium-high heat.

Stir in the bell pepper, garlic, lemon juice, tomato, pepper, stock, and salt.

Allow to simmer for 10 minutes while covered

Mix in the zucchini and parsley to cook for 12 minutes.

Set in serving bowls and enjoy

Nutrition Values:

Calories: 280, Fat: 8, Fiber: 3, Carbs: 5, Protein: 17

Pork Rolls

Preparation Time: 30 minutes

Servings: 6

Ingredients:

3 Peeled and minced garlic cloves

Italian seasoning - ½ teaspoon

6 prosciutto slices

Chopped fresh parsley - 2 tablespoons

Thinly sliced pork cutlets- 1 pound

Coconut oil - 1 tablespoon

Chopped onion- ¼ cup

Canned diced tomatoes - 15 ounces

Chicken stock - ⅓ cup

Grated Parmesan cheese - 2 tablespoons

Ricotta cheese- ⅓ cup e

Seasoning: Salt and ground black pepper

Directions:

Flatten pork pieces with a meat pounder.

Put prosciutto slices on top of each piece and then divide ricotta cheese, parsley, and Parmesan cheese.

Each piece of pork should be rolled and secure with a toothpick.

With medium-high temperature, heat the oil in a pan, add pork rolls, cook until brown on both sides, and transfer to a plate.

Heat the pan again over medium temperature, put onion and garlic, mix well. Cook for 5 minutes.

The stock should be added and cook for another 3 minutes.

Remove toothpicks from pork rolls and return into the pan.

Put tomatoes, Italian seasoning, salt, and pepper, bring to commotion by stirring, bring to a boil, reduce heat to medium-low, cover the pan with lid, and cook for 30 minutes.

Divide between plates and serve it.

Nutrition Values:

Calories: 256, Fat: 19, Fiber: 1, Carbs: 17, Protein: 12

Salad Bowl of CapreseWith Tomato

Preparation Time: 7 minutes

Servings: 3

Ingredients:

Mozzarella cheese-1/2 pound (sliced)

Balsamic vinegar-1 tablespoon

Olive oil-1 tablespoon

Tomato-1 (sliced)

Basil leaves-4 (torn)

Salt and black pepper-To taste

Instructions:

Settle the tomato and mozzarella slices alternatively.

Display on 2 plates. Season with the salt and pepper.

Drizzle the vinegar and olive oil. Sprinkle the basil leaves at the end.

Serve.

Nutrition :

Calories:- 150; Fat : 12; Fiber : 5; Carbs : 6; Protein : 9

Sauté Cabbage with Butter

Preparation and Cooking Time 20 minutes.

Servings: 4

Ingredients:

Green cabbage, shredded: 1½ pound

Salt: to taste

Ground black pepper: to taste

Unsalted butter: 5 ounces

Sweet paprika: 1/8 teaspoon

Directions:

Place a medium skillet pan over medium heat, add butter and when it melts, add cabbage.

Cook cabbage for 15 minutes, stirring often and then season with salt, black pepper, and paprika.

Continue cooking for 1 minute, then divide evenly between plates and serve.

Nutrition Values:

Calories: 805, Fat: 84, Fiber: 3, Carbs: 9, Protein: 1

Saute Edamame with Mint

Preparation and Cooking Time 10 minutes

Servings: 4

Ingredients:

Edamame: ¾ pound

Salt: to taste

Ground black pepper: to taste

Mint leaves, chopped: 1 tablespoon

Olive oil: 2 teaspoons

Green onions, chopped: 3

Minced garlic: ½ teaspoon

Directions:

Place a pan over medium heat, add oil and when hot, add edamame beans.

Season with salt and black pepper, then add remaining ingredients and stir until well mixed.

Cook edamame for 5 minutes until heated through, then divide evenly between serving plates and serve.

Nutrition Values:

Calories: 91, Fat: 3, Fiber: 4, Carbs: 17, Protein: 7

Sauteed Broccoli with Parmesan

Preparation Time: 32 minutes

Servings: 4

Ingredients:

broccoli florets - 1 pound

garlic clove - 1, minced

parmesan - 1 tablespoon, grated

olive oil - 5 tablespoons

Salt and black pepper to the taste.

Instructions:

Pour some water in a pot, then add a little salt and bring to a boil over medium high heat source.

Then add broccoli, cook for 5 minutes before removing the water.

Heat up a pan containing the oil over medium high heat source; then add garlic. Stir and cook for about 2 more minutes

Add broccoli; stir and cook for another 15 minutes

Remove the heat; sprinkle parmesan.

Divide into clean plates and serve

Nutrition :

Calories:- 193; Fat : 14; Fiber : 3; Carbs : 6; Protein : 5

Sautéed Kohlrabi with Parsley

Preparation and Cooking Time 15 minutes

Servings: 4

Ingredients:

Kohlrabi, trimmed and sliced thin: 2

Salt: to taste

Ground black pepper: to taste

Chopped parsley: 1 tablespoon

Unsalted butter: 1 tablespoon

Minced garlic: 1 teaspoon

Directions:

Place kohlrabi in a medium saucepan, pour in enough water to cover it, then place the pan over medium heat and bring to boil.

Then cook for 5 minutes, drain kohlrabi and transfer into a bowl.

Place a medium skillet pan over medium heat, add butter and when it melts, add garlic and cook for 1 minute or until fragrant.

Add kohlrabi, season with salt and black pepper and cook for 3 minutes per side or until nicely golden brown on both sides.

Add parsley, toss until mixed and remove pan from heat.

Divide kohlrabi evenly between serving plates and serve straight away.

Nutrition Values:

Calories: 55, Fat: 3, Fiber: 7, Carbs: 8, Protein: 9

Sautéed Mixed Vegetable with Pumpkin Seeds

Preparation and Cooking Time 10 minutes

Servings: 4

Ingredients:

Mushrooms, sliced: 14 ounces

Broccoli florets: 3 ounces

Red bell pepper, seeded and cut into strips: 3 ounces

Spinach, torn: 3 ounces

Garlic, minced: 2 tablespoons

Salt: to taste

Ground black pepper: to taste

Red pepper flakes: 1/8 teaspoon

Olive oil: 6 tablespoons

Pumpkin seeds: 2 tablespoons

Directions:

Place a skillet pan over medium-high heat, add oil and when hot, add garlic and cook for 1 minute or until fragrant.

Add mushrooms and cook for 3 minutes.

Then add broccoli florets and pepper, stir well, season with salt and black pepper, add pepper flakes and pumpkin seeds and cook for 3 minutes.

Add spinach, stir until just mixed, cook for 3 minutes and remove the pan from heat.

Serve straightaway.

Nutrition Values:

Calories: 271, Fat: 27, Fiber: 5, Carbs: 14, Protein: 6

Side Cauliflower Salad

Preparation Time: 15 minutes

Servings: 10

Ingredients:

Mayonnaise. 1 c

Salt

Chopped hard-boiled eggs, 4

Black pepper

Chopped celery, 1 cup.

Cauliflower florets, 21 oz.

Cider vinegar, 2 tbsps.

Erythritol, 1 tsp.

Water, 1 tbsp.

Chopped onion, 1 cup.

Directions:

Microwave the cauliflower florets with water in a heatproof bowl for 5 minutes

Set the salad in a bowl

Mix in the onions, celery, and eggs as you stir gently.

Combine salt, mayonnaise, pepper, vinegar, and erythritol in another bowl.

Add the mixture to the cauliflower, toss and enjoy.

Nutrition Values:

Calories: 139, Fat: 7, Fiber: 9, Carbs: 18, Protein: 8

Spicy Green Beans and Vinaigrette

Preparation Time: 22 minutes

Servings: 8

Ingredients:

Minced garlic clove, 1

Macadamia nut oil, 4 tbsps.

Lemon juice, 1 tsp.

Green beans, 2 lbs.

Smoked paprika, 2 tsps.

Salt

Chopped chorizo, 2 oz.

Black pepper

Coconut oil, 2 tbsps.

Coriander, ¼ tsp.

Beef stock, 2 tbsps.

Coconut vinegar, ½ cup.

Directions:

Put lemon juice, chorizo, vinegar, pepper, paprika, garlic, and salt in a blender to pulse until smooth.

Mix in macadamia nut oil and stock to blend again

Allow the coconut oil to melt over medium heat to sauté the green beans and chorizo mixture.

Cook for 10 minutes as you stir gently

Enjoy this wonderful meal

Nutrition Values:

Calories: 159, Fat: 11, Fiber: 1, Carbs: 8, Protein: 9

Stuffed Sausage with Bacon Wrappings

Preparation Time: 40 minutes

Servings: 4

Ingredients:

Onion powder

Bacon strips,

Salt.

Garlic powder.

Black pepper.

Sausages,

Sweet paprika, ½ tsp.

Pepper jack cheese slices, 1

Directions:

Ensure you have a medium high source of heat. Set a grill on it. Add sausages to cook until done all sides and set on a plate to cool.

Slice a pocket opening in the sausages. Each to be stuffed with 2 slices of pepper jack cheese. Apply a seasoning of onion, pepper, garlic powder, paprika and salt.

Each stuffed sausage should be wrapped in a bacon strip and grip using a toothpick. Set them on the baking sheet and transfer to the oven to bake at 400 0F for almost 15 minutes.

Serve immediately and enjoy.

Nutrition :

calories: 500, fat: 37, fiber: 12, carbs: 4, protein: 40

Tasty Lunch Pizza

Preparation Time: 17 minutes

Servings: 4

Ingredients:

Mascarpone cheese, ¼ cup.

Clive oil, 1 tbsp.

Shredded pizza cheese mix, 1 cup.

Ghee, 2 tbsps.

Heavy cream, 1 tbsp.

Lemon pepper

Shredded mozzarella cheese, 1 cup.

Steamed broccoli florets, 1/3 cup.

Salt.

Minced garlic, 1 tsp.

Black pepper.

Shaved asiago cheese

Directions:

Set the pan on fire to heat the oil to cook pizza mix then spread into a circle over medium heat

Spread the mozzarella cheese into a circle also

Allow everything to cook for 5 minutes and set on a plate

Set the pan on fire to melt the ghee for cooking lemon pepper, mascarpone cheese, cream, salt, pepper, and garlic for 5 minutes over medium heat.

Spread half of this mix over cheese crust.

Mix in broccoli florets to the pan with the remaining mascarpone mix to cook for 1 minute

Top the mixture on the pizza, sprinkle asiago cheese at the end and serve

Nutritional :

calories: 250, fat: 15, fiber: 1, carbs: 3, protein: 10

Turkey and Collard Greens Soup

Preparation and Cooking Time 2 hours and 30 minutes

Servings: 10

Ingredients:

Collard greens, chopped: 5 bunches

Salt: to taste

Ground black pepper: to taste

Red pepper flakes: 1 tablespoon

Chicken stock: 5 cups

Turkey leg: 1

Minced garlic: 2 tablespoons

Olive oil: ¼ cup

Directions:

Place a large pot over medium heat, add oil and when hot, add garlic.

Cook garlic for 1 minute, then turkey, season with salt and black pepper and then pout in stock.

Stir the mixture and simmer the soup for 30 minutes, covering the pot.

Add collard greens, stir until just mixed and cook for 45 minutes, covering the pot.

Then reduce heat to medium level, taste soup to adjust seasoning and continue cooking for 1 hour, covering the pot.

When done, take out greens from the soup using a slotted spoon, then take out the chicken and transfer to a cutting board.

Let the turkey cool for 10 minutes, then chop into bite size pieces and add into the soup.

Return greens into the soup, season with red pepper flakes and ladle evenly into serving bowls.

Serve immediately.

Nutrition Values:

Calories: 171, Fat: 19, Fiber: 8, Carbs: 2, Protein: 11

Warm Delicious Roasted Olives

Preparation Time: 30 minutes

Servings: 6

Ingredients:

kalamata olives - 1 cup, pitted

black olives - 1 cup, pitted

garlic cloves - 10

herbs de Provence - 1 tablespoon

lemon zest - 1 teaspoon, grated

green olives - 1 cup, stuffed with almonds and garlic

olive oil - 1/4 cup

Black pepper to the taste.

Some chopped thyme for serving

Instructions:

Spread black, kalamata and green olives on a lined baking sheet neatly, and drizzle some oil on them as well as on garlic and herbs de Provence,

Then toss to keep it well coated. Transfer into an oven set at a temperature of 425 0F and bake for 10 minutes

Stir the olives and bake for 10 another minutes.

Cut the olives on different plates, sprinkle lemon zest, black pepper and thyme on top.

Toss to ensure it is coated. Serve warm.

Nutrition :

Calories:- 200; Fat : 20; Fiber : 4; Carbs : 3; Protein : 1

Yummy Creamy Spaghetti Pasta: Side Dish

Preparation Time: 50 minutes

Servings: 4

Ingredients:

spaghetti squash - 1

ghee - 2 tablespoons

heavy cream - 2 cups

Cajun seasoning - 1 teaspoon

A pinch of cayenne pepper

Salt and black pepper to the taste.

Instructions:

Prick spaghetti with a fork, then arrange neatly on a lined baking sheet.

Move to an oven at 350 0F and bake for 15 minutes

Remove the spaghetti squash from the oven, keep it aside for a while and let it cool down. Scoop squash noodles

Heat up a pan containing ghee over medium heat; before adding spaghetti squash.

Then stir gently and cook for a couple of minutes

Sprinkle a pinch of salt, pepper, cayenne pepper and Cajun seasoning.

Then stir and cook for about a minute

Add heavy cream; stir, cook for 10 another 10 minutes.

Cut into different plates and serve as a keto side dish.

Nutrition :

Calories:- 200; Fat : 2; Fiber : 1; Carbs : 5; Protein : 8

Yummy Muffins

Preparation Time: 55 minutes

Servings: 13

Ingredients:

Egg yolks, 6

Coconut flour, ¾ cup.

Mushrooms, ½ lb.

Salt.

Ground beef, 1 lb.

Coconut aminos, 2 tbsps.

Directions:

Combine egg yolks, coconut aminos and salt in a blender. Process well until the desired consistency is attained.

In a separate bowl, stir in salt and beef. Stir in mushroom mixture to combine.

Stir in coconut flour.

Set the mixture into 13 cupcake cups and transfer into an oven preheated at 350 0F. bake the cups until done for 45 minutes

Allow to cool and enjoy your lunch

Nutritional :

calories: 160, fiber: 3, carbs: 1, fat: 10, protein: 12

Zucchini and Squash Noodles with Peppers

Preparation and Cooking Time 30 minutes

Servings: 6

Ingredients:

Medium zucchinis, cut with a spiralizer: 1 ½

Medium summer squash, cut with a spiralizer: 1

Butternut squash, cut with a spiralizer: 4 ounce

Medium white onion, peeled and chopped: 4 ounces

Mixed bell peppers, seeded and cut into thin strips: 6 ounces

Minced garlic: 1 ½ teaspoon

Salt: to taste

Ground black pepper: to taste

Bacon fat: 4 tablespoons

Directions:

Set oven to 400 0F and let preheat.

In the meantime, place zucchini noodles on a baking sheet lined with parchment paper and then add onion and bell peppers.

Add garlic, season with salt and black pepper and toss until evenly coated.

Add bacon fat, toss until coated and place the baking sheet into an oven.

Bake for 20 minutes or until done and serve straightaway.

Nutrition Values:

Calories: 179, Fat: 6, Fiber: 6, Carbs: 19, Protein: 10

Baked Potato Mix

Preparation time: 10 mins

Cooking time: one hour and quarter-hour

Servings: 8

Ingredients:

6 potatoes, peeled and sliced

2 garlic cloves, minced

2 tablespoons organic olive oil

1 and ½ cups coconut cream

¼ cup coconut milk

1 tablespoon thyme, chopped

¼ teaspoon nutmeg, ground

A pinch of red pepper flakes

1 and ½ cups low-fat cheddar, shredded

½ cup low-fat parmesan, grated

Directions:

Heat up a pan with all the oil over medium heat, add garlic, stir and cook for 1 minute.

Add coconut cream, coconut milk, thyme, nutmeg and pepper flakes, stir, bring which has a simmer, reduce heat to low and cook for 10 mins.

Arrange 1/3 with all the potatoes in a very baking dish, add 1/3 with the cream, repeat with the rest through the potatoes along with the cream, sprinkle the cheddar for the top, cover with tin foil, introduce within the oven and cook at 375 degrees F for 45 minutes.

Uncover the dish, sprinkle the parmesan, bake everything for 20 mins, divide between plates and serve as as being a side dish.

Enjoy!

Nutrition Values: calories 224, fat 8, fiber 9, carbs 16, protein 15

Spicy Brussels sprouts

Preparation time: ten mins

Cooking time: 20 minutes

Servings: 6

Ingredients:

2 pounds Brussels sprouts, halved

2 tablespoons essential extra virgin olive oil

A pinch of black pepper

1 tablespoon sesame oil

2 garlic cloves, minced

½ cup coconut aminos

2 teaspoons apple cider vinegar treatment

1 tablespoon coconut sugar

2 teaspoons chili sauce

A pinch of red pepper flakes

Sesame seeds for serving

Directions:

Spread the sprouts over the lined baking dish, add the primary essential olive oil, the sesame oil, black pepper, garlic, aminos, vinegar, coconut sugar, chili sauce and pepper flakes, toss well, introduce within the oven and bake at 425 degrees F for twenty minutes.

Divide the sprouts between plates, sprinkle sesame seeds at the very top and serve as a side dish.

Enjoy!

Nutrition Values: calories 176, fat 3, fiber 6, carbs 14, protein 9

Baked Cauliflower

Preparation time: ten minutes

Cooking time: half an hour

Servings: 4

Ingredients:

3 tablespoons organic extra virgin olive oil

2 tablespoons chili sauce

Juice of a single lime

3 garlic cloves, minced

1 cauliflower head, florets separated

A pinch of black pepper

1 teaspoon cilantro, chopped

Directions:

In a bowl, combine the oil while using chili sauce, lime juice, garlic and black pepper and whisk.

Add cauliflower florets, toss, spread on the lined baking sheet, introduce inside oven and bake at 425 degrees F for a half-hour.

Divide the cauliflower between plates, sprinkle cilantro at the top and serve as being a side dish.

Enjoy!

Nutrition Values: calories 188, fat 4, fiber 7, carbs 14, protein 8

Baked Broccoli

Preparation time: ten minutes

Cooking time: quarter-hour

Servings: 4

Ingredients:

1 tablespoon organic olive oil

1 broccoli head, florets separated

2 garlic cloves, minced

½ cup coconut cream

½ cup low-fat mozzarella, shredded

¼ cup low-fat parmesan, grated

A pinch of pepper flakes, crushed

Directions:

In a baking dish, combine the broccoli with oil, garlic, cream, pepper flakes and mozzarella and toss.

Sprinkle the parmesan on top, introduce inside the oven and bake at 375 degrees F for fifteen minutes.

Divide between plates and serve as a side dish.

Enjoy!

Nutrition Values: calories 188, fat 4, fiber 7, carbs 14, protein 7

Easy Slow Cooked Potatoes

Preparation time: 10 mins

Cooking time: 6 hours

Servings: 6

Ingredients:

Cooking spray

2 pounds baby potatoes, quartered

3 cups low-fat cheddar cheese, shredded

2 garlic cloves, minced

8 bacon slices, cooked and chopped

¼ cup green onions, chopped

1 tablespoon sweet paprika

A pinch of black pepper

Directions:

Spray a pokey cooker while using cooking spray, add baby potatoes, cheddar, garlic, bacon, green onions, paprika and black pepper, toss, cover and cook on High for 6 hours.

Divide between plates and serve being a side dish.

Enjoy!

Nutrition Values: calories 200, fat 4, fiber 6, carbs 12, protein 7

Mashed Potatoes

Preparation time: 10 minutes

Cooking time: 20 mins

Servings: 6

Ingredients:

3 pounds potatoes, peeled and cubed

2 tablespoons non-fat butter

½ cup coconut milk

A pinch of salt and black pepper

½ cup low-fat sour cream

Directions:

Put the potatoes in the pot, add water to purchase, put in a pinch of salt and pepper, bring with a boil over medium heat, cook for twenty or so minutes and drain.

Add butter, milk and sour cream, mash well, stir everything, divide between plates and serve as a side dish.

Enjoy!

Nutrition Values: calories 188, fat 3, fiber 7, carbs 14, protein 8

Avocado Side Salad

Preparation time: ten mins

Cooking time: 0 minutes

Servings: 4

Ingredients:

4 blood oranges, peeled and cut into segments

2 tablespoons extra virgin olive oil

A pinch of red pepper, crushed

2 avocados, peeled, pitted and cut into wedges

1 and ½ cups baby arugula

¼ cup almonds, toasted and chopped

1 tablespoon fresh freshly squeezed lemon juice

Directions:

In a bowl, combine the oranges while using oil, red pepper, avocados, arugula, almonds and fresh lemon juice, toss, divide between plates and serve as being a side dish.

Enjoy!

Nutrition Values: calories 231, fat 4, fiber 8, carbs 16, protein 6

Classic Side Dish Salad

Preparation time: ten mins

Cooking time: 0 minutes

Servings: 4

Ingredients:

3 garlic cloves, minced

Juice of ½ lemon

6 ounces coconut cream

2 lettuce hearts, torn

1 cup corn

4 ounces green beans, halved

1 cup cherry tomatoes, halved

1 cucumber, chopped

1/3 cup chives, chopped

1 avocado, peeled, pitted and halved

6 bacon slices, cooked and chopped

Directions:

In a bowl, combine the lettuce with corn, green beans, cherry tomatoes, cucumber, chives, avocado and bacon and toss.

In another bowl, combine the garlic with fresh fresh lemon juice and coconut cream, whisk well, add towards the salad, toss and serve as a side dish.

Enjoy!

Nutrition Values: calories 175, fat 12, fiber 4, carbs 13, protein 6

Easy Kale Mix

Preparation time: ten mins

Cooking time: 0 minutes

Servings: 4

Ingredients:

1 wheat grains bread slice, toasted and torn into small pieces

6 tablespoons low-fat cheddar, grated

3 tablespoons extra virgin olive oil

5 tablespoons fresh lemon juice

1 garlic herb, minced

7 cups kale, torn

A pinch of black pepper

Directions:

In a bowl, combine the bread with cheese and kale.

In another bowl, combine the oil with all the freshly squeezed lemon juice, garlic and black pepper, whisk, add towards the salad, toss, divide between plates and serve as as a side dish.

Enjoy!

Nutrition Values: calories 200, fat 4, fiber 5, carbs 14, protein 8

Asparagus Salad

Preparation time: ten mins

Cooking time: 4 minutes

Servings: 4

Ingredients:

4 tablespoons avocado oil

2 tablespoons balsamic vinegar

1 tablespoon coconut aminos

1 garlic herb, minced

1 pound asparagus, trimmed

6 cups frisee lettuce leaves, torn

1 cup edamame, shelled

1 cup parsley, chopped

Directions:

Heat up a pan with 1 tablespoon oil over medium-high heat, add asparagus, cook for 4 minutes and transfer which has a salad bowl.

Add lettuce, edammae and parsley and toss.

In another bowl, combine the remaining from your oil when using vinegar, aminos and garlic, whisk well, add inside the salad, toss, divide between plates and serve as being a side dish.

Enjoy!

Nutrition Values: calories 200, fat 4, fiber 5, carbs 14, protein 6

Green Side Salad

Preparation time: 10 minutes

Cooking time: 0 minutes

Servings: 4

Ingredients:

4 cups baby spinach leaves

1 cucumber, sliced

3 ounces broccoli florets

3 ounces green beans, blanched and halved

¾ cup edamame, shelled

1 and ½ cups green grapes, halved

1 cup orange juice

¼ cup extra virgin organic olive oil

1 tablespoon cider vinegar

2 tablespoons parsley, chopped

2 teaspoons mustard

A pinch of black pepper

Directions:

In a salad bowl, combine a baby spinach with cucumber, broccoli, green beans, edamame and grapes and toss.

Add orange juice, organic extra virgin olive oil, vinegar, parsley, mustard and black pepper, toss well, divide between plates and serve as a side dish.

Enjoy!

Nutrition Values: calories 117, fat 4, fiber 5, carbs 14, protein 4

Baked Zucchini

Preparation time: ten mins

Cooking time: 20 minutes

Servings: 4

Ingredients:

4 zucchinis, quartered lengthwise

½ teaspoon thyme, dried

½ teaspoon oregano, dried

½ cup low-fat parmesan, grated

½ teaspoon basil, dried

¼ teaspoon garlic powder

2 tablespoons essential olive oil

2 tablespoons parsley, chopped

A pinch of black pepper

Directions:

Arrange zucchini pieces having a lined baking sheet, add thyme, oregano, basil, garlic powder, oil, parsley and black pepper and toss well.

Sprinkle parmesan ahead, introduce within the oven and bake at 350 degrees F for twenty roughly minutes.

Divide between plates and serve as a side dish.

Enjoy!

Nutrition Values: calories 198, fat 4, fiber 4, carbs 14, protein 5

Chapter 11 : Dinner Recipes

Biryani

Servings: 6

Preparation Time: 15 minutes

Cooking Time: 15 minutes

Total Time: 30 minutes

Ingredients

Black pepper as desired

Sea salt as desired

Garam masala .5 tsp

Coconut oil 1 tsp

Shelled peas 1 c

Water 5 c

Coriander .5 tsp ground

Chili powder 1 tsp

Turmeric 5 tsp

Carrots 2 quartered

Potatoes 2 quartered

Bay leaves 2 torn

Cumin seeds .5 tsp

Onion 1 sliced thin

Vegetable oil 3 T

White rice long grain 2 c

Directions

Add the rice to a large pot and cover it with three to four inches of water before allowing it to soak for about 20 minutes. Drain and set aside.

Add the oil to your pressure cooker and set it over medium heat. Add in the onion, bay leaves, and cumin seeds and let everything cook about 5 minutes until the onion is nearly see through.

Mix in the carrots and potatoes and let them cook an additional 5 minutes and the potatoes have begun to brown. Add in the coriander, turmeric and chili powder and let everything cook 1 additional minute.

Add the rice to the pressure cooker and ensure it is well covered in the boil before adding in the peas and water. Mix in the garam masala, oil, and salt before sealing the cooker and turning it to high pressure. Let everything cook for 5 minutes before removing from heat.

Allow the pressure to naturally release and fluff the rice with a fork prior to serving.

Autumn Roasted Green Beans

Servings: 4

Preparation Time: 15 minutes

Cooking Time: 30 minutes

Total Time: 45 minutes

Ingredients

Walnuts .5 c toasted

Cranberries .5 c dried

Black pepper as desired

Kosher sea salt as desired

Lemon juice 2 tsp.

Lemon zest 1 tsp.

Sugar .25 tsp.

Coconut oil 2 T

Garlic 4 cloves, quartered and peeled

Green beans 2 lbs. stems trimmed

Directions

Preheat your oven to 350F and crack and smash the walnuts into chunks.

Spread the walnuts onto a baking sheet and toast them for 10 minutes.

Increase the temperature on the oven to 450F.

Cover a baking sheet with a rim using aluminum foil.

In a mixing bowl, combine the sugar, pepper, salt and coconut oil before coating the garlic and green beans thoroughly.

Place the beans onto a baking sheet and spread them out to ensure they cook well. Place the sheet into the oven and let the beans bake for 15 minutes, before stirring with a spatula and roasting another 10 minutes.

Mix in the lemon juice, pepper and salt prior to serving.

Zoodles

Servings: 2

Preparation Time: 5 minutes

Cooking Time: 0 minutes

Total Time: 5 minutes

Ingredients

Zucchini 4 organic

Directions- Zoodle Creation

If you have access to a spiralizer, use it to create noodles of zucchini. If you do not own a spiralizer, this recipe is still very simple. Just slice the zucchini into long thin strips. You may also wish to use a cheese and vegetable grater to get the desired noodle effect.

Serve the zoodles as they are or let them boil for two minutes in a pan of water to warm them up and soften them a bit. Alternately, you may wish to sauté them in a bit of coconut oil or Coconut oil for a minute or two to give them a little crispness.

Serve the zoodles in place of the traditional noodles in your favorite pasta dishes.

Roasted Rosemary Potatoes

Servings: 6

Preparation Time: 10 minutes

Cooking Time: 25 minutes

Total Time: 35 minutes

Ingredients

Garlic 1 head

Rosemary 3 sprigs

Thyme 3 sprigs

Baby potatoes 20 oz.

Parsley 2 T chopped

Sea salt as desired

Black pepper as desired

Coconut oil 2 T

Directions

Ensure your oven is heated to 450F.

Separate garlic cloves and remove the papery skin holding them together, but do not peel.

Add the rosemary, thyme, baby potatoes, parsley, garlic, and coconut oil together in a large bowl, coating well.

Add the results to a jelly roll pan that has been lined with tinfoil before topping with pepper and salt. Place the pan in the oven and let the potatoes bake approximately 25 minutes, stirring at the 12-minute mark.

Season with additional pepper and salt prior to serving.

Sweet Potato Wedges

Servings: 6

Preparation Time: 10 minutes

Cooking Time: 30 minutes

Total Time: 40 minutes

Ingredients

Salt 1 tsp.

Cracked black pepper 1 tsp.

Garlic powder .5 tsp.

Sweet potatoes 4 medium, peeled, each cut into 6 wedges

Rosemary 1 T chopped, fresh

Coconut oil 2 T

Directions

Preheat oven to 450F.

In a mixing bowl, combine the coconut oil, rosemary, sweet potatoes, garlic powder, black pepper, and salt together and ensure the potatoes are coated well.

Add the results in a single layer to a large roasting pan before placing the pan in the oven and letting the potatoes bake for 20 minutes. Turn the dish at this point before baking another 10 minutes.

Best Lentil Curry

Servings: 4

Preparation Time: 10 min

Cooking Time: 30 minutes

Total Time: 40 minutes

Ingredients

Vegetable broth 4 c low sodium

Red lentil 1 c

Potato 10 oz. peeled and made into pieces that are 1 inch each

Carrot 8 oz. chopped

Curry powder 1 T

Scallions 8 separated, sliced

Garlic 2 cloves chopped

Ginger 2 T chopped

Coconut oil 3 T

Directions

•Add the oil to a saucepan before placing it on the stove on top of a burner set to a high/medium heat.

•Add in the scallion whites, garlic and ginger and let them soften for 2 minutes.

•Mix in the curry powder as well as pepper and salt, as desired, broth, lentils, potato, and carrots before letting everything boil. Turn down the heat and let everything simmer for 15 minutes, stirring regularly.

•Top with scallion greens prior to serving.

Parmesan sprinkled garlic beans

Preparation Time: 20 minutes

Servings: 4

Ingredients:

Trimmed green beans- 1½ Ib.

Olive oil- 3 tbsp.

Minced garlic cloves- 4

Grated parmesan: 2 tbsp.

Red pepper flakes- ½ tsp.

Directions:

Cover beans with water in a pot and simmer over medium-high for 5 minutes.

Remove the water and set aside in a bowl.

Pour oil in a an over medium-high and add pepper flakes, garlic, and beans an cook for 6 minutes.

Serve topped with parmesan.

Nutrition Values:

Calories 200, carbs 11, protein 6, fiber 6, fats 3

Lamb & Pineapple Kebabs

One of the delicious recipe of lamb and pineapple kebabs with a tasty layer of char... Fresh mint gives a refreshing touch to these kebabs.

Servings: 4-6

Preparation Time: 15 minutes

Cooking Time: 10 minutes

Ingredients:

1 large pineapple, cubed into 1½-inch size, divided

1 (½-inch) piece fresh ginger, chopped

2 garlic cloves, chopped

Salt, to taste

16-24-ounce lamb shoulder steak, trimmed and cubed into 1½-inch size

Fresh mint leaves from a bunch

Ground cinnamon, to taste

Directions:

In a food processor, add about 1½ cups of pineapple, ginger, garlic and salt and pulse till smooth.

Transfer the mixture into a large bowl.

Add chops and coat with mixture generously.

Refrigerate to marinate for about 1-2 hours.

Preheat the grill to medium heat. Grease the grill grate.

Thread lam, remaining pineapple and mint leaves onto pre-soaked wooden skewers.

Grill the kebabs for about 10 minutes, turning occasionally.

Baked Meatballs & Scallions

A recipe of lamb meatballs that is filled with flavor and aroma... Baked meatballs pair nicely with the crispy tips of braised scallions.

Servings: 4-6

Preparation Time: 20 minutes

Cooking Time: 35 minutes

Ingredients:

For Meatballs:

1 lemongrass stalk, outer skin peeled and chopped

1 (1½-inch) piece fresh ginger, sliced

3 garlic cloves, chopped

1 cup fresh cilantro leaves, chopped roughly

½ cup fresh basil leaves, chopped roughly

2 tablespoons plus 1 teaspoon fish sauce

2 tablespoons water

2 tablespoons fresh lime juice

½ pound lean ground pork

1 pound lean ground lamb

1 carrot, peeled and grated

1 organic egg, beaten

For Scallions:

16 stalks scallions, trimmed

2 tablespoons coconut oil, melted

Salt, to taste

½ cup water

Directions:

Preheat the oven to 375 degrees F. Grease a baking dish.

In a food processor, add lemongrass, ginger, garlic, fresh herbs, fish sauce, water and lime juice and pulse till chopped finely.

Transfer the mixture into a bowl with remaining ingredients and mix till well combined.

Make about 1-inch balls from mixture.

Arrange the balls into prepared baking dish in a single layer.

In another rimmed baking dish, arrange scallion stalks in a single layer.

Drizzle with coconut oil and sprinkle with salt.

Pour water in the baking dish 1nd with a foil paper cover it tightly.

Bake the scallion for about 30 minutes.

Bake the meatballs for about 30-35 minutes.

Roasted Brussels Sprouts

Servings: 4

Preparation Time: 5 minutes

Cooking Time: 15 minutes

Total Time: 20 minutes

Ingredients

Sea salt .25 tsp.

Black pepper .25 tsp.

Brussel sprouts .75lbs. sliced in half length-wise

Coconut oil 5 T.

Directions

Ensure your oven is heated to 400F. Cut Brussels sprouts in half and place in a medium-sized bowl. Drizzle the coconut oil over the Brussels sprouts and then toss with the sea salt and black pepper until evenly coated.

Pour Brussels sprouts onto a baking sheet and make sure they are evenly spaced so that they will roast easily.

Place the sheet in the oven and let it cook approximately 10 minutes before stirring well and returning it to the oven for 10 minutes more. Season as desired They will keep in the fridge for 3-4 days, or in the freezer for 2-3 months.

Pork with Bell Pepper

This stir fry not only tastes wonderful but also is packed with nutritious benefits. Fresh lime juice intensifies the flavor of this stir fry.

Servings: 4

Preparation Time: 15 minutes

Cooking Time: 13 minutes

Ingredients:

1 tablespoon fresh ginger, chopped finely

4 garlic cloves, chopped finely

1 cup fresh cilantro, chopped and divided

¼ cup plus 1 tbsp olive oil, divided

1 pound tender pork, trimmed, sliced thinly

2 onions, sliced thinly

1 green bell pepper, seeded and sliced thinly

1 tablespoon fresh lime juice

Directions:

In a large bowl, mix together ginger, garlic, ½ cup of cilantro and ¼ cup of oil.

Add pork and coat with mixture generously.

Refrigerate to marinate for about 2 hours.

Heat a large skillet on medium-high heat.

Add pork mixture and stir fry for about 4-5 minutes.

Transfer the pork into a bowl.

In the same skillet, heat remaining oil on medium heat.

Add onion and sauté for about 3 minutes.

Stir in bell pepper and stir fry for about 3 minutes.

Stir in pork, lime juice and remaining cilantro and cook for about 2 minutes.

Serve hot.

Roasted Summer Squash

Servings: 4

Preparation Time: 5 minutes

Cooking Time: 30 minutes

Total Time: 35 minutes

Ingredients

Zucchini 3

Yellow squash 3

Kosher salt 5 T

Black pepper .5 T

Coconut oil 2 T

Directions

Ensure your oven is heated to 400F

Peel vegetables and cut into.25 inch thick slices.

Assemble vegetables on a baking sheet or pan and drizzle coconut oil on top. Sprinkle with seasoning as desired

Bake at 400F for 30 minutes.

Savory Baked Acorn Squash

Servings: 4

Preparation Time: 5 minutes

Cooking Time: 30 minutes

Total Time: 35 minutes

Ingredients

Acorn squash 1

Kosher salt as desired

Black pepper as desired

Coconut oil 2 tsp.

Smoked paprika as desired

Directions

Ensure your oven is heated to 425F.

Cut acorn squash in half lengthwise, then cut halves into quarters lengthwise. Scoop out seeds and discard.

Place the squash on baking sheet and drizzle coconut oil over the top of each quarter. Scatter with the smoked paprika, salt, and pepper and bake in the oven for 30 minutes.

Pork with Pineapple

A wonderfully delicious recipe which will surely impress a meat lover… Pineapple compliments pork tenderloin in a wonderful way.

Servings: 4

Preparation Time: 15 minutes

Cooking Time: 14 minutes

Ingredients:

2 tablespoons coconut oil

1½ pound pork tenderloin, trimmed and cut into bite-sized pieces

1 onion, chopped

2 minced garlic cloves

1 (1-inch) piece fresh ginger, minced

20-ounce pineapple, cut into chunks

1 large red bell pepper, seeded and chopped

¼ cup fresh pineapple juice

¼ cup coconut aminos

Salt and freshly ground black pepper, to taste

Directions:

In a large skillet, melt coconut oil on high heat.

Add pork and stir fry for about 4-5 minutes.

Transfer the pork into a bowl.

In the same skillet, heat remaining oil on medium heat.

Add onion, garlic and ginger and sauté for about 2 minutes.

Stir in pineapple and bell pepper and stir fry for about 3 minutes.

Stir in pork, pineapple juice and coconut aminos and cook for about 3-4 minutes.

Serve hot.

Caraway Pork Mix

Preparation time: ten mins

Cooking time: 40 minutes

Servings: 6

Ingredients:

2 pounds pork meat, boneless and cubed

2 yellow onions, chopped

1 tablespoon extra-virgin extra virgin olive oil

1 garlic cloves, minced

3 cups low-sodium chicken stock

2 tablespoons sweet paprika

1 teaspoon caraway seeds

Black pepper towards taste

2 tablespoons parsley, chopped

Directions:

Heat up a pot while using the oil over medium heat, add pork and brown it for 10 minutes.

Add onions, garlic, stock, caraway seeds, paprika and pepper, provide your boil, reduce temperature, cover and cook for half an hour.

Add parsley, toss, divide into bowls and serve.

Enjoy!

Nutrition Values: calories 310, fat 4, fiber 4, carbs 13, protein 15

Roasted Mixed Olives

Preparation and Cooking Time 40 minutes

Servings: 6

Ingredients:

Black olives, pitted: 1 cup

Kalamata olives, pitted: 1 cup

Green olives, stuffed with almonds and garlic: 1 cup

Garlic cloves, peeled: 10

Olive oil: ¼ cup

Herbes de Provence: 1 tablespoon

Lemon zest, grated: 1 teaspoon

Ground black pepper: to taste

Chopped thyme, for serving: ½ teaspoon

Directions:

Set oven to 425 0F and let preheat.

In the meantime, place all olives on a baking sheet lined with parchment paper, then add garlic and herbes de Provence, drizzle with oil and toss until coated.

Place the baking sheet into the oven and bake for 10 minutes.

Then add olives and continue baking for 20 minutes, stirring halfway through.

When done, divide olives evenly between serving plates, season with black pepper, sprinkle with lemon zest and thyme and toss until evenly coated.

Serve immediately.

Nutrition Values:

Calories: 189, Fat: 13, Fiber: 5, Carbs: 4, Protein: 5

Rolls of Sausage Pizzas

Preparation Time: 40 minutes

Servings: 6

Ingredients:

Pizza sauce, ¼ cup.

Shredded mozzarella cheese, 2 cup.

Cooked sausage, ½ cup.

Salt.

Pizza seasoning, 1 tsp.

Chopped onion, 2 tbsps.

Black pepper.

Chopped red and green bell peppers, ¼ cup.

Chopped tomato,

Directions:

Line a baking sheet. Grease it slightly. Over the sheet, spread mozzarella cheese and top with sprinkles of pizza seasoning. Set in an oven preheated to 400 0F and bake until done for 20 minutes.

Remove the pizza crust from the oven. Spread it with tomatoes, sausage, bell peppers and onion. Top with tomato sauce drizzling.

Take back to the oven and bake for another 10 minutes.

Remove the pizza from oven and allow to cool. Slice into 6 equal parts and roll. Enjoy your lunch.

Nutrition :

calories: 117, fiber: 1, carbs: 2, fat: 7, protein: 11

Lamb Burgers with Avocado Dip

A winner and delicious burger recipe for whole family... These burgers are great when with smooth and silky textured avocado dip.

Servings: 4-6

Preparation Time: 20 minutes

Cooking Time: 10 minutes

Ingredients:

For Burgers:

1 (2-inch) piece fresh ginger, grated

1 pound lean ground lamb

1 medium onion, grated

2 minced garlic cloves

1 bunch fresh mint leaves, chopped finely

2 teaspoons ground coriander

2 teaspoons ground cumin

½ teaspoon ground allspice

½ teaspoon ground cinnamon

Salt and freshly ground black pepper, to taste

1 tbsp olive oil

For Dip:

3 small cucumbers, peeled and grated

1 avocado, peeled, pitted and chopped

½ of garlic clove, crushed

2 tablespoons fresh lemon juice

2 tablespoons olive oil

2 tablespoons fresh dill, chopped finely

2 tablespoons chives, chopped finely

Salt and freshly ground black pepper, to taste

Directions:

Preheat the broiler of oven. Lightly, grease a broiler pan.

For burgers in a large bowl, squeeze the juice of ginger.

Add remaining ingredients and mix till well combined.

Make equal sized burgers from the mixture.

Arrange the burgers in broiler pan and broil for about 5 minutes per side.

Meanwhile for dip squeeze the cucumbers juice in a bowl.

In a food processor, add avocado, garlic, lemon juice and oil and pulse till smooth.

Transfer the avocado mixture in a bowl.

Add remaining ingredients and stir to combine.

Serve the burgers with avocado dip.

Mustard Pork Chops

Preparation time: ten mins

Cooking time: twenty minutes

Servings: 6

Ingredients:

2 pork chops

¼ cup organic essential olive oil

2 yellow onions, sliced

2 garlic cloves, minced

2 teaspoons mustard

1 teaspoon sweet paprika

Black pepper towards taste

½ teaspoon oregano, dried

Directions:

In a tiny bowl, mix oil with garlic, mustard, paprika, black pepper, and oregano and whisk well.

Add the pork chops, toss well leave aside to 10 mins.

Place the meat for the preheated grill over medium-high heat and cook for 10 minutes on both sides.

Divide pork chops between plates and serve employing a side salad.

Enjoy!

Nutrition Values: calories 314, fat 4, fiber 4, carbs 7, protein 17

Greek Mixed Roasted Vegetables

Servings: 4

Preparation Time: 15 minutes

Cooking Time: 45 minutes

Total Time: 60 minutes

Ingredients- Vegetables

1 eggplant peeled and diced .75-inch

Black pepper as desired

Kosher sea salt as desired

Extra virgin olive oil 2 T

Garlic 2 cloves minced

Onion 1 peeled, diced 1-inch

Bell pepper 2 red, yellow, diced, 1-inch

Ingredients- Dressing

Coconut oil .25 c

Lemon juice .3 c squeezed fresh

Black pepper as desired

Kosher sea salt as desired

Basil 15 leaves

Scallions 4 minced

Directions

Ensure your oven is heated to 425F.

One a sheet pan, combine the garlic, onion, yellow bell pepper, red bell pepper, and eggplant before seasoning using the pepper, salt, and coconut oil.

Add the pan to the oven and let it cook for 40 minutes, using a spatula to flip everything after 20 minutes.

As the vegetables are cooking, combine the pepper, salt, coconut oil, and lemon juice together in a small bowl, add the results to the vegetables as soon as they are ready.

Let the pan cool completely before adding in the basil, feta, and scallions. Season prior to serving.

Pork and Lentils Soup

Preparation time: ten mins

Cooking time: an hour and 5 minutes

Servings: 6

Ingredients:

1 small yellow onion, chopped

1 tablespoon olive oil

1 and ½ teaspoons basil, chopped

1 and ½ teaspoons ginger, grated

3 garlic cloves, chopped

Black pepper for the taste

1 carrot, chopped

1 pound pork chops, boneless and cubed

3 ounces brown lentils, rinsed

3 cups low sodium chicken stock

2 tablespoons tomato paste

2 tablespoons lime juice

Directions:

Heat up a pot with all the current oil over medium heat, add garlic, onion, basil, ginger, carrots and black pepper, stir and cook for 10 mins.

Add the pork and brown for 5 minutes more.

Add lentils, tomato paste and stock, bring with a boil, cover pot and simmer for 50 minutes.

Add lime juice, toss, ladle into bowls and serve.

Enjoy!

Nutrition Values: calories 273, fat 4, fiber 6, carbs 12, protein 16

Pork and Veggies Stew

Preparation time: 10 mins

Cooking time: 60 minutes and 10 minutes

Servings: 4

Ingredients:

½ cup low-sodium chicken stock

1 tablespoon ginger, grated

1 teaspoon coriander, ground

2 teaspoons cumin, ground

Black pepper for that taste

2 and ½ pounds pork butt, cubed

28 ounces canned tomatoes, no-salt-added, drained and chopped

4 ounces carrots, chopped

1 red onion, cut into wedges

4 garlic cloves, minced

15 ounces canned chickpeas, no-salt-added, drained and rinsed

1 tablespoon cilantro, chopped

Directions:

Heat up a pot over medium heat, add pork cubes and brown the crooks to minutes.

Add ginger, coriander, cumin, black pepper, onion, carrots and garlic, stir and cook for 5 minutes more.

Add the stock, the tomatoes also since the chickpeas, toss, bring to a simmer, cover the pot and cook for an hour.

Add cilantro, stir, divide into bowls and serve.

Enjoy!

Nutrition Values: calories 256, fat 6, fiber 8, carbs 12, protein 24

Pork and Snow Peas Salad

Preparation time: ten mins

Cooking time: 0 minutes

Servings: 4

Ingredients:

1 red chili, chopped

2 tablespoons balsamic vinegar

1/3 cup coconut aminos

1 tablespoon lime juice

1 teaspoon extra virgin olive oil

4 ounces mixed salad greens

4 ounces snow peas, blanched

1 red bell pepper, sliced

4 ounces pork, cooked and cut into thin strips

Directions:

In a salad bowl, mix greens with peas, bell pepper and pork..

Add the chili, vinegar, aminos, lime juice and oil, toss well and serve.

Enjoy!

Nutrition Values: calories 235, fat 4, fiber 4, carbs 12, protein 17

Pork and Beans Stew

Preparation time: twenty roughly minutes

Cooking time: 1 hour and ten mins

Servings: 4

Ingredients:

2 pounds pork butt, trimmed and cubed

1 and ½ tablespoons essential extra virgin olive oil

2 eggplants, chopped

1 yellow onion, chopped

1 red bell pepper, chopped

3 garlic cloves, minced

1 tablespoon thyme, dried

2 teaspoons sage, dried

4 ounces canned white beans, no-salt-added, drained and rinsed

1 cup low-sodium chicken stock

12 ounces zucchinis, chopped

2 tablespoons tomato paste

Directions:

Heat up a pot with all the oil over medium-high heat, add pork and brown for 5 minutes.

Add the onion, garlic, thyme, sage, bell pepper and eggplants, toss and cook for 5 minutes more.

Add beans, stock and tomato paste, toss, bring to a simmer, cover the pot and cook for 50 minutes.

Add the zucchinis, toss, cook for ten mins more, divide into bowls and serve.

Enjoy!

Nutrition Values: calories 310, fat 3, fiber 5, carbs 12, protein 22

Spiced Pork

One of the absolute delicious dish of spiced pork... Slow cooking helps to infuse the spice flavors in pork very nicely.

Servings: 6

Preparation Time: 15 minutes

Cooking Time: 1 hour 52 minutes

Ingredients:

1 (2-inch) piece fresh ginger, chopped

5-10 garlic cloves, chopped

1 teaspoon ground cumin

½ teaspoon ground turmeric

1 tablespoon hot paprika

1 tablespoon red pepper flakes

Salt, to taste

2 tablespoons cider vinegar

2 pounds pork shoulder, trimmed and cubed into 1½-inch size

2 cups hot water, divided

1 (1-inch wide) ball tamarind pulp

¼ cup olive oil

1 teaspoon black mustard seeds, crushed

4 green cardamoms

5 whole cloves

1 (3-inch) cinnamon stick

1 cup onion, chopped finely

1 large red bell pepper, seeded and chopped

Directions:

In a food processor, add ginger, garlic, cumin, turmeric, paprika, red pepper flakes, salt and cider vinegar and pulse till smooth.

Transfer the mixture into a large bowl.

Add pork and coat with mixture generously.

Keep aside, covered for about 1 hour at room temperature.

In a bowl, add 1 cup of hot water and tamarind and keep aside till water becomes cool.

With your hands, crush the tamarind to extract the pulp.

Add remaining cup of hot water and mix till well combined.

Through a fine sieve, strain the tamarind juice in a bowl.

In a large skillet, heat oil on medium-high heat.

Add mustard seeds, green cardamoms, cloves and cinnamon stick and sauté for about 4 minutes.

Add onion and sauté for about 5 minutes.

Add pork and stir fry for about 6 minutes.

Stir in tamarind juice and bring to a boil.

Reduce the heat to medium-low and simmer 1½ hours.

Stir in bell pepper and cook for about 7 minutes.

Pork Chili

A great bowl of healthy chili with an amazing addition of bokchoy. This healthy chili is tasty, spicy and refreshing at the same time.

Servings: 8

Preparation Time: 15 minutes

Cooking Time: 1 hour

Ingredients:

2 tablespoons extra-virgin olive oil

2 pound ground pork

1 medium red bell pepper, seeded and chopped

1 medium onion, chopped

5 garlic cloves, chopped finely

1 (2-inch) piece of hot pepper, minced

1 tablespoon ground cumin

1 teaspoon ground turmeric

3 tablespoon chili powder

½ teaspoon chipotle chili powder

Salt and freshly ground black pepper, to taste

1 cup chicken broth

1 (28-ounce) can fire-roasted crushed tomatoes

2 medium bokchoy heads, sliced

1 avocado, peeled, pitted and chopped

Directions:

In a large pan, heat oil on medium heat.

Add pork and stir fry for about 5 minutes.

Add bell pepper, onion, garlic, hot pepper and spices and stir fry for about 5 minutes.

Add broth and tomatoes and bring to a boil.

Stir in bokchoy and cook, covered for about 20 minutes.

Uncover and cook for about 20-30 minutes.

Serve hot with the topping of avocado.

Ground Pork with Water Chestnuts

This recipe is an easy way to prepare weeknight meal with a healthy touch... This recipe prepares a flavor packed meal.

Servings: 4

Preparation Time: 15 minutes

Cooking Time: 12 minutes

Ingredients:

1 tablespoon plus 1 teaspoon coconut oil

1 tablespoon fresh ginger, minced

1 bunch scallion (white and green parts separated), chopped

1 pound lean ground pork

Salt, to taste

1 tablespoon 5-spice powder

1 (18-ounce) can water chestnuts, drained and chopped

1 tablespoon organic honey

2 tablespoons fresh lime juice

Directions:

In a large heavy bottomed skillet, heat oil on high heat.

Add ginger and scallion whites and sauté for about ½-1½ minutes.

Add pork and cook for about 4-5 minutes.

Drain the excess fat from skillet.

Add salt and 5-spice powder and cook for about 2-3 minutes.

Add scallion greens and remaining ingredients and cook, stirring continuously for about 1-2 minutes.

Nutrition Values:

Calories: 520

Fat: 30g

Sat Fat: 6g

Carbohydrates: 37g

Fiber: 4g

Sugar: 9g

Protein: 25g

Sodium: 950mg

Glazed Pork chops with Peach

One of an easy and impressive way to enjoy pork and fresh peach in a delicious glaze... This sweet and spicy glaze makes pork super delicious.

Servings: 2

Preparation Time: 15 minutes

Cooking Time: 16 minutes

Ingredients:

2 boneless pork chops

Salt and freshly ground black pepper, to taste

1 ripe yellow peach, peeled, pitted, chopped and divided

1 tbsp olive oil

2 tablespoons shallot, minced

2 tablespoons garlic, minced

2 tablespoons fresh ginger, minced

1 tablespoon organic honey

1 tablespoon balsamic vinegar

1 tablespoon coconut aminos

¼ teaspoon red pepper flakes, crushed

¼ cup water

Directions:

Sprinkle the pork chops with salt and black pepper generously.

In a blender, add half of peach and pulse till a puree forms.

Reserve remaining peach.

In a skillet, heat oil on medium heat.

Add shallots and sauté for about 1-2 minutes.

Add garlic and ginger and sauté for about 1 minute.

Add remaining ingredients and reduce the heat to medium-low.

Bring to a boil and simmer for about 4-5 minutes or till a sticky glaze forms.

Remove from heat and reserve 1/3 of the glaze and keep aside.

Coat the chops with remaining glaze.

Heat a nonstick skillet on medium-high heat.

Add chops and sear for about 4 minutes from both sides.

Transfer the chops in a plate and coat with the remaining glaze evenly.

Top with reserved chopped peach and serve.

Pork chops in Creamy Sauce

Pork chops with extra twist of delish flavors... This special and easy technique of coconut sauce gives extra flavor and texture to pork chops.

Servings: 4

Preparation Time: 15 minutes

Cooking Time: 14 minutes

Ingredients:

2 garlic cloves, chopped

1 small jalapeño pepper, chopped

¼ cup fresh cilantro leaves

1½ teaspoons ground turmeric, divided

1 tablespoon fish sauce

2 tablespoons fresh lime juice

1 (13½-ounce) can coconut milk

4 (½-inch thick) pork chops

Salt, to taste

1 tablespoon coconut oil

1 shallot, chopped finely

Directions:

In a blender, add garlic, jalapeño pepper, cilantro, 1 teaspoon of ground turmeric, fish sauce, lime juice and coconut milk and pulse till smooth.

Sprinkle the pork with salt and remaining turmeric evenly.

In a skillet, melt butter on medium-high heat.

Add shallots and sauté for about 1 minute.

Add chops and cook for about 2 minutes per side.

Transfer the chops in a bowl.

Add coconut mixture and bring to a boil.

Reduce the heat to medium and simmer, stirring occasionally for about 5 minutes.

Stir in pork chops and cook for about 3-4 minutes.

Serve hot.

Baked Pork & Mushroom Meatballs

A healthy, hearty and tasty recipe of meatballs…. Fresh herbs add a really refreshing and aromatic touch in these baked meatballs.

Servings: 6

Preparation Time: 15 minutes

Cooking Time: 15 minutes

Ingredients:

1 pound lean ground pork

1 organic egg white, beaten

4 fresh shiitake mushrooms, stemmed and minced

1 tablespoon fresh parsley, minced

1 tablespoon fresh basil leaves, minced

1 tablespoon fresh mint leaves, minced

2 teaspoons fresh lemon zest, grated finely

1½ teaspoons fresh ginger, grated finely

Salt and freshly ground black pepper, to taste

Directions:

Preheat the oven to 425 degrees F. Arrange the rack in the center of oven.

Line a baking sheet with a parchment paper.

In a large bowl, add all ingredients and mix till well combined.

Make small equal-sized balls from mixture.

Arrange the balls onto prepared baking sheet in a single layer.

Bake for about 12-15 minutes or till done completely.

Chapter 12: Snacks Recipes

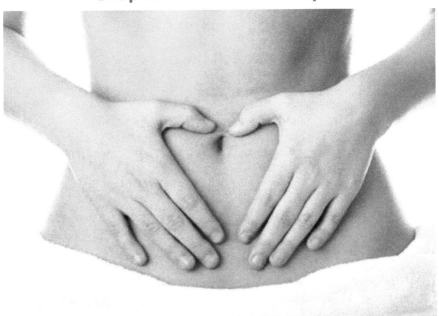

Chickpeas and Pepper Hummus

Preparation time: ten mins

Cooking time: 0 minutes

Servings: 4

Ingredients:

14 ounces canned chickpeas, no-salt-added, drained and rinsed

1 tablespoon sesame paste

2 roasted red peppers, chopped

Juice of ½ lemon

4 walnuts, chopped

Directions:

In your blender, combine the chickpeas with all the sesame paste, red peppers, lemon juice and walnuts, pulse well, divide into bowls and serve as as being a snack.

Enjoy!

Nutrition Values: calories 231, fat 12, fiber 6, carbs 15, protein 14

Lemony Chickpeas Dip

Preparation time: 10 mins

Cooking time: 0 minutes

Servings: 4

Ingredients:

14 ounces canned chickpeas, drained, no-salt-added, rinsed

Zest of merely one lemon, grated

Juice of a single lemon

1 tablespoon olive oil

4 tablespoons pine nuts

½ cup coriander, chopped

Directions:

In a blender, combine the chickpeas with lemon zest, freshly squeezed lemon juice, coriander and oil, pulse well, divide into small bowls, sprinkle pine nuts at the pinnacle and serve as a conference dip.

Enjoy!

Nutrition Values: calories 200, fat 12, fiber 4, carbs 9, protein 7

Chili Nuts

Preparation time: 10 minutes

Cooking time: 10 mins

Servings: 4

Ingredients:

½ teaspoon chili flakes

1 egg white

½ teaspoon curry powder

½ teaspoon ginger powder

4 tablespoons coconut sugar

A pinch of cayenne

14 ounces mixed nuts

Directions:

In a bowl, combine the egg white with all the chili flakes, curry powder, curry powder, ginger powder, coconut sugar and cayenne and whisk well.

Add the nuts, toss well, spread them having a lined baking sheet, introduce within the oven and bake at 400 degrees F for ten mins.

Divide the nuts into bowls and serve as a snack.

Enjoy!

Nutrition Values: calories 234, fat 12, fiber 5, carbs 14, protein 7

Protein Bars

Preparation time: ten mins

Cooking time: 0 minutes

Servings: 4

Ingredients:

4 ounces apricots, dried

2 ounces water

2 tablespoons rolled oats

1 tablespoon sunflower seeds

2 tablespoons coconut, shredded

1 tablespoon sesame seeds

1 tablespoon cranberries

3 tablespoons hemp seeds

1 tablespoon chia seeds

Directions:

In your food processor, combine the apricots while using water along with all the oats, pulse well, transfer for your bowl, add coconut, sunflower seeds, sesame seeds, cranberries, hemp and chia seeds and stir prior to getting a paste.

Roll this inside a log, wrap, cool inside fridge, slice and serve as a snack.

Enjoy!

Nutrition Values: calories 100, fat 3, fiber 4, carbs 8, protein 5

Eggplant, Olives and Basil Salad

Preparation Time: 15 minutes

Servings 4

Ingredients:

Tomatoes, chopped: 1 ½ cups

Eggplant, cubed: 3 cups

Capers: 2 teaspoons

Green olives, pitted and sliced: 6 ounces

Minced garlic: 2 teaspoons

Salt: ½ teaspoon

Ground black pepper: ¼ teaspoon

Chopped basil: 1 tablespoon

Olive oil: 2 teaspoons

Balsamic vinegar: 2 teaspoons

Directions:

Place a medium skillet pan over medium-high heat, add oil and when hot, add eggplant pieces and cook for 5 minutes.

Then add remaining ingredients, stir well and cook for 5 minutes.

When done, remove the pan from heat and let cool for 5 minutes.

Then divide salad evenly between small cups and serve as an appetizer.

Nutrition Values:

calories: 199, fat: 6, fiber: 5, carbs: 7, protein: 7

Fresh Tomato, Onion and Jalapeno Pepper Salsa

Preparation Time: 5 minutes

Servings 4

Ingredients:

Cherry tomatoes, halved: 2 cups

Red onion, peeled and chopped: ¼ cup

Jalapeno pepper, chopped: 1

Minced garlic: ½ teaspoon

Chopped cilantro: 2 tablespoons

Salt: ¼ teaspoon

Ground black pepper: ¼ teaspoon

Lime juice: 2 tablespoons

Directions:

Place all the ingredients for salsa in a medium bowl and stir until combined.

Serve straight away as a snack.

Nutrition Values:

calories: 87, fat: 1, fiber: 2, carbs: 7, protein: 5

Fresh Veggie Bars

Preparation Time: 40 minutes

Servings: 18

Ingredients:

Egg-1

Broccoli florets-2 cups

Cheddar cheese-1/3 cup (grated)

Onion-¼ cup (peeled and chopped)

Cauliflower rice-½ cup

Fresh parsley-2 tablespoons (chopped)

Olive oil-A drizzle (for greasing)

Salt and black pepper-to taste (ground)

Directions:

Warm up a saucepan with water over medium heat

Stir into the broccoli and let it simmer for a minute.

Strain and finely chop it to put into a bowl.

Mix in the egg, cheddar cheese, cauliflower rice, salt, pepper, parsley, and mix.

Give them the shape of bars by using the mixture on your hands.

Put them on a greased baking sheet.

Keep it in an oven at 400ºF and bake for 20 minutes.

Settle the prepared dish on a platter to serve.

Nutrition Values:

Calories: 19, Fat: 1, Fiber: 3, Carbs: 3, Protein: 3

Green Beans And Avocado with Chopped Cilantro

Preparation Time: 15 minutes

Servings: 4

Ingredients:

Avocados: 2; pitted and peeled

green beans - 2/3 pound, trimmed

scallions - 5, chopped.

olive oil - 3 tablespoons

A handful cilantro, chopped.

Salt and black pepper to the taste.

Directions:

Heat up a pan containing oil on a medium-high heat source; then add green beans and stir gently. Cook this mixture for about 4 minutes

Add salt and pepper to the pan; and stir gently, then remove the heat and move to a clean bowl.

Mix the avocados with salt and pepper and mash with a fork inside a clean bowl.

Then add onions and stir properly.

Add this over green beans, then toss to ensure it is well coated.

Finally, serve with some chopped cilantro on top.

Nutrition :

Calories:- 200; Fat : 5; Fiber : 3; Carbs : 4; Protein : 6

Italian Pizza Dip

Preparation Time: 30 minutes

Servings: 4

Ingredients:

Italian seasoning, ½ tsp.

Black pepper

Mozzarella cheese, ½ cup.

Chopped green bell pepper, 1 tbsp.

Sour cream, ¼ cup.

Salt

Grated Parmesan cheese, ¼ cup.

Tomato sauce, ½ cup.

Mayonnaise, ¼ cup.

Softened cream cheese, 4 oz.

Chopped pepperoni slices, 6

Chopped black olives, 4

Directions:

Gently stir together pepper, sour cream, cream cheese, mayonnaise, mozzarella cheese, and salt in a big bowl

Put the mixture into four ramekins then top with tomato sauce, parmesan cheese, then bell pepper, pepperoni, Italian seasoning, and black olives

Set your oven for 20 minutes at 350oF

Allow to bake

Enjoy the meal warm.

Nutrition Values:

Calories: 284, Fat: 24, Fiber: 1, Carbs: 5, Protein: 6

Jalapeno Cheesy Balls

Preparation Time: 10 minutes

Servings: 2

Ingredients:

Cream cheese, 3 oz.

Garlic powder, ¼ tsp.

Onion powder, ¼ tsp.

Black pepper

Chopped jalapeno peppers, 2

Salt

Dried parsley, ½ tsp.

Cooked and crumbled bacon slices, 3

Directions:

Set the mixing bowl in position to combine garlic powder, bacon, seasonings, parsley, and onion with the jalapeno peppers

Shape the mixture into balls

Set the balls on a flat plate to take as a cold appetizer

Nutrition Values:

Calories: 200, Fat: 5, Fiber: 4, Carbs: 12, Protein: 6

Keto Veggie Noodles: Side Dish

Preparation Time: 30 minutes

Servings: 6

Ingredients:

Zucchini - 1, cut with a spiralizer

summer squash - 1, cut with a spiralizer

yellow, orange and red bell peppers - 6 ounces; cut into thin strips

bacon fat - 4 tablespoons

garlic cloves - 3, minced

carrot - 1, cut with a spiralizer

sweet potato - 1, cut with a spiralizer

red onion - 4 ounces, chopped.

Salt and black pepper to the taste.

Directions:

Arrange zucchini noodles neatly on a lined baking sheet.

Then add squash, carrot, sweet potato, onion and all bell peppers

Sprinkle a pinch of salt, pepper and garlic and toss to coat.

Then add bacon fat, toss again all noodles.

Move to an oven set at a temperature of 400 oF and bake for about 20 minutes

Move to clean plates. Serve immediately as a keto side dish.

Nutrition :

Calories:- 50; Fat : 1; Fiber : 1; Carbs : 6; Protein : 2

Minty Zucchini Rolls

Preparation Time: 20 minutes

Servings: 24

Ingredients:

Chopped basil, ¼ cup.

Sliced zucchinis, 3

Ricotta cheese, 1 1/3 cup.

Salt

Chopped mint, 2 tbsps.

Black pepper

Basil leaves, 24

Olive oil, 2 tbsps.

Directions:

Prepare the baking tray by lining well.

Add the zucchini slices then splash the oil and the seasonings on it

Set the oven for 10 minutes at 3750F, allow to bake

Meanwhile, set the mixing bowl in position to stir together chopped basil, ricotta, seasonings, and mint.

Divide the mixture on the zucchini slices as you roll

Set the rolls on a flat plate

Enjoy

Nutrition Values:

Calories: 172, Fat: 3, Fiber: 4, Carbs: 9, Protein: 4

Sesame Zucchini Spread

Preparation Time: 16 minutes

Servings: 4

Ingredients:

Lemon juice, ½ cup.

Veggie stock, 3 tbsps.

Olive oil, ¼ cup.

Salt

Chopped zucchinis, 4 cup.

Black pepper

Minced garlic cloves, 4

Sesame seeds paste, ¾ cup.

Directions:

Set your pan over medium-high heat with half of the oil to cook the garlic and zucchini for two minutes

Stir in the seasonings and stock to cook for four minutes

Move the zucchinis to the blender with the remaining oil, lemon juice, and sesame seeds paste to process until smooth.

Set the mixture in bowls to serve

Enjoy.

Nutrition Values:

Calories: 140, Fat: 5, Fiber: 3, Carbs: 6, Protein: 7

Shrimp Salad with Tomato and Radish

Preparation Time: 10 minutes

Servings 8

Ingredients:

Shrimp, cooked, peeled and deveined: 1 pound

Medium white onion, chopped: ¼ cup

Tomato, cubed: 1

Radishes, chopped: 4

Minced jalapeno: 1 ½ teaspoon

Salt: ¼ teaspoon

Ground black pepper: ¼ teaspoon

Lime juice: 2 tablespoons

Chopped cilantro: ¼ cup

Directions:

Place all the ingredients for the salad in a medium bowl and stir until combined.

Serve salad straightaway as an appetizer.

Nutrition Values:

calories: 90, fat: 1, fiber: 1, carbs: 2, protein: 6

Shrimp wrapped with prosciutto

Preparation Time: 30 minutes

Servings: 16

Ingredients:

Red wine, 1/3 cup.Chopped mint, 1 tbsp.

Erythritol, 2 tbsps.

Cooked shrimp, 10 oz.

Olive oil, 2 tbsps.

Blackberries, 1/3 cup.

Sliced prosciutto 11

Directions:

Have the shrimp well wrapped with prosciutto slices.

Arrange the wrapped shrimp in a baking sheet then sprinkle with olive oil

Set the oven for 15 minutes at 4250F then allow to bake.

In the meantime, heat the mashed blackberries over medium heat.

Stir in erythritol, mint, and wine.

Set the shrimp on a serving plate, top the blackberries sauce and enjoy.

Nutrition Values:

Calories: 89, Fat: 5, Fiber: 2, Carbs: 1, Protein: 11

Simple Tomato Tarts

Preparation Time: 1 hour 20 minutes

Servings: 12

Ingredients:

Salt

Olive oil, ¼ cup.

Black pepper

Sliced tomatoes, 2

For the base:

Coconut flour, 2 tbsps.

Psyllium husk, 1 tbsp.

Butter, 5 tbsps.

Almond flour, ½ cup.

Salt

For the filling:

Sliced onion, 1Chopped thyme, 3 tsps.

Olive oil, 2 tbsps.

Minced garlic, 2 tbsps.

Crumbled goats cheese, 3 oz.

Directions:

Season the tomato slices then align on a baking sheet then dazzle some olive oil.

Set your oven for 40 minutes at 4250F.

Allow to bake

On the other hand, combine cold butter, coconut flour, pepper, almond flour, salt, psyllium husk in a food processor to achieve a dough.

Divide dough into silicone cupcake molds, press.

Set the oven for 20 minutes at 3500F then allow to bake.

Once fully baked, remove from oven and reserve.

Remove the tomato slices from the oven and allow them to cool

Top the tomato slices on the cupcakes

Meanwhile, quick fry the onions in a pan over medium-high heat, for about four minutes.

Stir in thyme and garlic, for about one minute.

Spread mixture on top of tomato slices.

Sprinkle the goat cheese on top.

Set your oven for 5 minutes at 350 oF

Bake until the cheese melts away

Enjoy

Nutrition Values:

Calories: 125, Fat: 17, Fiber: 1, Carbs: 1, Protein: 9

Special Tomato AndBocconcini: Side Dish

Preparation Time: 6 minutes

Servings: 4

Ingredients:

babybocconcini - 8 ounces, drain and torn

basil leaves - 1 cup, roughly chopped.

Tomatoes - 20 ounces, cut in wedges

stevia - 1 teaspoon

garlic clove - 1, finely minced

extra virgin olive oil - 2 tablespoons

balsamic vinegar - 1½ tablespoons

Salt and black pepper to the taste.

Directions:

Mix stevia with vinegar, garlic, oil, salt and pepper in a bowl and whisk very well.

Add bocconcini with tomato and basil to a clean salad and mix.

Add dressing, toss to keep well coated

Serve immediately as a keto side dish.

Nutrition Values:

Calories:- 100; Fat : 2; Fiber : 2; Carbs : 1; Protein : 9

Stir-Fried Queso

Preparation Time: 20 minutes

Servings: 6

Ingredients:

Olive oil, 1 ½ tbsps.

Cubed Queso Blanco, 5 oz.

Chopped olives, 2 oz.

Red pepper flakes

Directions:

Set up the pan to heat the oil over medium-high heat to cook the Queso cubes

Turn the Queso cubes using a spatula then sprinkle with olives

Allow the cubes to cook more for 5 minutes then turn again to sprinkle with red pepper flake.

Allow to cook to a crispy texture.

Turn the cubes again to cook on the other side

Once cooked, set on the chopping board then slice into small pieces

Enjoy.

Nutrition Values:

Calories: 152, Fat: 18, Fiber: 3, Carbs: 6, Protein: 2

Potato Chips

Preparation time: ten mins

Cooking time: 30 minutes

Servings: 6

Ingredients:

2 gold potatoes, cut into thin rounds

1 tablespoon olive oil

2 teaspoons garlic, minced

Directions:

In a bowl, combine the french fries while using the oil along with the garlic, toss, spread more than a lined baking sheet, introduce inside the oven and bake at 400 degrees F for a half-hour.

Divide into bowls and serve.

Enjoy!

Nutrition Values: calories 200, fat 3, fiber 5, carbs 13, protein 6

Peach Dip

Preparation time: ten mins

Cooking time: 0 minutes

Servings: 2

Ingredients:

½ cup nonfat yogurt

1 cup peaches, chopped

A pinch of cinnamon powder

A pinch of nutmeg, ground

Directions:

In a bowl, combine the yogurt while using the peaches, cinnamon and nutmeg, whisk, divide into small bowls and serve being a snack.

Enjoy!

Nutrition Values: calories 165, fat 2, fiber 3, carbs 14, protein 13

Cereal Mix

Preparation time: 10 mins

Cooking time: 40 minutes

Servings: 6

Ingredients:

3 tablespoons extra virgin organic olive oil

1 teaspoon hot sauce

½ teaspoon garlic powder

½ teaspoon onion powder

½ teaspoon cumin, ground

A pinch of red pepper cayenne

3 cups rice cereal squares

1 cup cornflakes

½ cup pepitas

Directions:

In a bowl, combine the oil while using the hot sauce, garlic powder, onion powder, cumin, cayenne, rice cereal, cornflakes and pepitas, toss, spread on the lined baking sheet, introduce inside the oven and bake at 350 degrees F for 40 minutes.

Divide into bowls and serve as a snack.

Enjoy!

Nutrition Values: calories 199, fat 3, fiber 4, carbs 12, protein 5

Easy Tuna Cakes

Preparation Time: 18 minutes

Servings: 12

Ingredients:

A drizzle of olive oil

Medium eggs, 3

Dried parsley, 1 tsp.

Garlic powder, 1 tsp.

Salt

Chopped red onion, ½ cup.

Black pepper

Canned tuna, 15 oz.

Directions:

Set a mixing bowl in position to stir together parsley, seasonings, eggs, garlic powder, and onion then mold the mixture into patties.

Set a pan on fire with the oil to cook the cakes evenly over medium-high heat.

Set the patties on a serving platter and enjoy as an appetizer

Nutrition Values:

Calories: 160, Fat: 2, Fiber: 4, Carbs: 6, Protein: 6

Mushrooms Stuffed with shrimp mixture.

Preparation Time: 30 minutes

Servings: 5

Ingredients:

Cooked shrimp, 1 cup.

Garlic powder, 1 tsp.

Salt

Chopped onion, 1

Chopped white mushroom caps, 24 oz.

Black pepper

Softened cream cheese, 4 oz.

Mayonnaise, ¼ cup.

Sour cream, ¼ cup.

Curry powder, 1 tsp.

Quesoblanco or Monterey Jack cheese, ½ cup.

Directions:

Set the mixing bowl in a working surface.

Whisk in onion, mayonnaise, shrimp, curry powder, Mexican cheese, Pepper, cream cheese, garlic powder, salt, and sour cream.

Fill the mushrooms with the combination and set on a baking tray

Set your oven for 20 minutes at 350oF, allow too bake

Enjoy the meal once fully baked

Nutrition Values:

Calories: 259, Fat: 18, Fiber: 9, Carbs: 17, Protein: 16

Oven-baked Crackers

Preparation Time: 25 minutes

Servings: 6

Ingredients:

Ghee, 3 tbsps.

Salt

Minced garlic clove, 1

Black pepper

Dried basil, ¼ tsp.

Baking powder, ½ tsp.

Basil pesto, 2 tbsps.

Almond flour, 1¼ cup.

Directions:

Set the mixing bowl in position to combine the almond flour, seasonings, basil pesto, baking powder, ghee, and the garlic to make a dough

Line the baking tray then set the dough on it.

Set the oven for 17 minutes at 3250F, allow to bake

Slice into medium crackers the moment they are cold then serve them as a snack.

Enjoy

Nutrition Values:

Calories: 200, Fat: 20, Fiber: 1, Carbs: 4, Protein: 7

Parmesan Spinach Balls

Preparation Time: 22 minutes

Servings: 30

Ingredients:

Whipping cream, 3 tbsps.

Grated Parmesan cheese, 1/3 cup.

Medium eggs, 2

Crumbled feta cheese, 1/3 c

Almond flour, 1 cup.

Spinach, 16 oz.

Salt

Melted butter, 4 tbsps.

Ground nutmeg, ¼ tsp.

Black pepper

Onion powder, 1 tbsp.

Garlic powder, 1 tsp.

Directions:

Plug in and set your food processor in position

Add in feta cheese, spinach, nutmeg, eggs, whipping cream, garlic powder, almond flour, pepper, butter, onion, and salt.

Process until smooth. Pour the mixture in a bowl to refrigerate in the freezer for 10 minutes.

Mold into 30 spinach balls and set them on a well-greased baking tray. Set your oven for 12 minutes at 350 0F, allow to bake thoroughly.

Allow the balls to cool and enjoy

Nutrition Values:

Calories: 40, Fat: 5, Fiber: 5, Carbs: 1, Protein: 7

Pecan with Maple syrup Bars

Preparation Time: 35 minutes

Servings: 12

Ingredients:

Maple syrup, ¼ cup.

Stevia, ¼ tsp.

Crushed pecans, toasted, 2 cup.

Almond flour, 1 cup.

Coconut oil, ½ cup.

Flaxseed meal, ½ cup.

Shredded coconut, ½ cup.

For the maple syrup:

Vanilla extract, ½ tsp.

Coconut oil, 2 ¼ tbsp.

Xanthan gum, ¼ tsp.

Erythritol, ¼ cup.

Water, ¾ cup.

Maple extract, 2 tsps.

Butter, 1 tbsp.

Directions:

Microwave 2¼ teaspoon coconut oil, butter, xanthan gum, in a heatproof bowl for about one minute.

Mix in maple, erythritol, vanilla extract, and water as you stir gently.

Microwave again for another one minute.

Meanwhile, combine coconut flour, flaxseed meal, and almond flour in another bowl as you stir gently.

Stir in the pecans then add coconut oil, ¼ cup maple syrup, and stevia.

Set the mixture in a baking sheet

Set your oven for 25 minutes at 3500F then allow to bake.

Allow cooling before slicing and serving.

Nutrition Values:

Calories: 313, Fat: 31, Fiber: 3, Carbs: 18, Protein: 7

Plum and Jalapeno Salad with Basil

Preparation Time: 10 minutes

Servings 6

Ingredients:

Plums, chopped: 1 cup

Chopped basil: 2 tablespoons

Jalapeno pepper, chopped: 1

Red onion, peeled and chopped: 2 tablespoons

Lime juice: 2 teaspoons

Salt: ½ teaspoon

Ground black pepper: ¼ teaspoon

Stevia: 2 tablespoons

Ground cumin: ½ teaspoon

Olive oil: 1 teaspoon

Directions:

Place all the ingredients for the salad in a medium bowl and stir until combined.

Place salad bowl in a refrigerator for 1 hour or until chilled and then serve as an appetizer.

Nutrition Values:

calories: 137, fat: 2, fiber: 2, carbs: 7, protein: 5

Seasoned Easy Fried Cabbage

Preparation Time: 25 minutes

Servings: 4

Ingredients:

green cabbage - 1½ pound, shredded

ghee - 5 ounces

A pinch of sweet paprika

Salt and black pepper to the taste.

Directions:

Add heat to a pan containing ghee over medium-high heat source.

Then pour some cabbage to the pan and cook for 15 minutes stirring frequently.

Then sprinkle a pinch of salt, pepper and paprika.

Stir gently, cook for another minute

Divide into different plates

Now you can serve

Nutrition :

Calories:- 200; Fat : 4; Fiber : 2; Carbs : 3;
Protein : 7

Tasty Avocado Spread

Preparation Time: 1 minute

Servings: 4

Ingredients:

Stevia, ¼ tsp.

Halved avocados, 2

Juice of 2 limes

Coconut milk, 1 cup.

Chopped cilantro, ½ cup.

Zest of 2 limes

Directions:

Plug and switch on the blender in position.

Add in the stevia, avocados, lime juice, coconut milk,
and cilantro, and lime zest to process until smooth.

Set into serving bowls to enjoy

Nutrition Values:

Calories: 190, Fat: 6, Fiber: 2, Carbs: 9, Protein: 6

Red Pepper Muffins

Preparation time: ten minutes

Cooking time: half an hour

Servings: 12

Ingredients:

1 and ¾ cups whole wheat grains flour

2 teaspoons baking powder

2 tablespoons coconut sugar

A pinch of black pepper

1 egg

¾ cup almond milk

2/3 cup roasted red pepper, chopped

½ cup low-fat mozzarella, shredded

Directions:

In a bowl, combine the flour with baking powder, coconut sugar, black pepper, egg, milk, red pepper and mozzarella, stir well, divide in a very lined muffin tray, introduce in the oven and bake at 400 degrees F for a half-hour.

Serve like a snack.

Enjoy!

Nutrition Values: calories 149, fat 4, fiber 2, carbs 14, protein 5

Nuts and Seeds Mix

Preparation time: 10 mins

Cooking time: 0 minutes

Servings: 6

Ingredients:

1 cup pecans

1 cup hazelnuts

1 cup almonds

¼ cup coconut, shredded

1 cup walnuts

½ cup papaya pieces, dried

½ cup dates, dried, pitted and chopped

½ cup sunflower seeds

½ cup pumpkin seeds

1 cup raisins

Directions:

In a bowl, combine the pecans with all the hazelnuts, almonds, coconut, walnuts, papaya, dates, sunflower seeds, pumpkin seeds and raisins, toss and serve as a snack.

Enjoy!

Nutrition Values: calories 188, fat 4, fiber 6, carbs 8, protein 6

Tortilla Chips

Preparation time: ten mins

Cooking time: 25 minutes

Servings: 6

Ingredients:

12 whole wheat grains grains tortillas, cut into 6 wedges each

2 tablespoons organic extra virgin olive oil

1 tablespoon chili powder

A pinch of cayenne

Directions:

Spread the tortillas for the lined baking sheet, add the oil, chili powder and cayenne, toss, introduce inside oven and bake at 350 degrees F for 25 minutes.

Divide into bowls and serve as as a side dish.

Enjoy!

Nutrition Values: calories 199, fat 3, fiber 4, carbs 12, protein 5

Kale Chips

Preparation time: ten mins

Cooking time: fifteen minutes

Servings: 8

Ingredients:

1 bunch kale leaves

1 tablespoon organic olive oil

1 teaspoon smoked paprika

A pinch of black pepper

Directions:

Spread the kale leaves over a baking sheet, add black pepper, oil and paprika, toss, introduce inside oven and bake at 350 degrees F for quarter-hour.

Divide into bowls and serve being a snack.

Enjoy!

Nutrition Values: calories 177, fat 2, fiber 4, carbs 13, protein 6

Pan-Fried Cheesy Sticks

Preparation Time: 1 hour 30 minutes

Servings: 16

Ingredients:

Black pepper

Mozzarella string cheese pieces, 8

Whisked eggs, 2

Italian seasoning, 1 tbsp.

Olive oil, ½ cup.

Grated Parmesan cheese, 1 cup.

Minced garlic clove, 1

Salt

Directions:

Set a medium mixing bowl on a clean working area.

Stir together salt, Italian seasoning, parmesan cheese, pepper, and garlic

In another mixing bowl, place the whisked eggs then coat the mozzarella sticks in egg mixture then cheese mixture.

Repeat the process twice to coat well then freeze for an hour.

After one hour, heat the oil in a pan over medium-high heat to fry the sticks to a golden color evenly

Set on a platter and enjoy

Nutrition Values:

Calories: 116, Fat: 14, Fiber: 0, Carbs: 8, Protein: 8

546. Pan-fried Italian Meatballs

Preparation Time: 16 minutes

Servings: 16

Ingredients:

Chopped basil, 2 tbsps.

Salt

Chopped sundried tomatoes, 2 tbsps.

Black pepper

Almond flour, ¼ cup.

Large egg, 1Ground turkey, 1 lb.

Shredded mozzarella cheese, ½ cup.

Garlic powder, ½ tsp.

Olive oil, 2 tbsps.

Directions:

Set your medium size mixing bowl in a clean working surface

Stir together the egg, ground turkey, garlic powder, pepper, basil, salt, mozzarella, almond flour, and sun-dried tomatoes

Mold the mixture into12 even meatballs

Set the pan over medium-high heat to melt the oil

Fry the meatballs in the oil until browned

Enjoy

Nutrition Values:

Calories: 81, Fat: 5, Fiber: 1, Carbs: 5, Protein: 5

Parmesan Basil Dip

Preparation Time: 5 minutes

Servings 10

Ingredients:

Chopped basil: 1 tablespoon

Minced garlic: ½ teaspoon

Lemon juice: 1 teaspoon

Basil pesto: 2 tablespoons

Avocado mayonnaise: 1 cup

Grated parmesan cheese: 1 tablespoon

Directions:

Place all the ingredients for the dip in a medium bowl and stir until combined.

Divide dip evenly between small bowls and serve.

Nutrition Values:

calories: 100, fat: 4, fiber: 2, carbs: 5, protein: 3

Parmesan Chicken Wings

Preparation Time: 34 minutes

Servings: 6

Ingredients:

Medium egg, 1 Black pepper

Italian seasoning, ½ tsp.

Butter, 2 tbsps.

Salt

Halved chicken wings, 6 lbs.

Grated Parmesan cheese, ½ cup.

Red pepper flakes, ¼ tsp.

Garlic powder, 1 tsp.

Directions:

Line the baking tray well and arrange the wings.

Set the oven for 17 minutes at 425 0F. Allow to bake.

Meanwhile, plug in and set the food processor in position.

Add in the Italian seasoning, butter, salt, garlic powder, cheese, red pepper flakes, egg, and pepper. Blend to mix well

Once the oven timer beeps, remove the wings and turn them.

Set the oven to broil

Allow the chicken wings to broil for 5 minutes

Remove the wings to coat with sauce over

Broil again for one minute.

Enjoy.

Nutrition Values:

Calories: 677, Fat: 51, Fiber: 0, Carbs: 1, Protein: 52

Chapter 13: Healthy and Delicious Beverages

Citrus Flavored Water

Time: 20 minutes

Serving Size: 4

Ingredients:

I 1 cup of sliced lemons

I ½ cup of sliced limes

I 1 cup of sliced oranges

I 2 cups of diced watermelon

I 1 cup of sliced cucumbers

I A pitcher of cold water

Directions:

1. Add all the fruit to the pitcher of water.

2. Stir well to incorporate the flavors.

3. Refrigerate the mixture for several hours before serving.

Basil-Infused Tomato Water

Time: 5 minutes

Serving Size: 4

Ingredients:

l 1 diced red tomato

l 3 branches of crushed basil

l A pitcher of cold water

Directions:

1. Add the tomato and basil to the pitcher of water.

2. Stir well to incorporate the flavors.

3. Refrigerated for at least two hours to allow the fruit flavor to infuse the water. Strain and serve chilled. This can be refrigerated up to two days.

Refreshing Strawberry

Time: 5 minutes

Serving Size: 6

Ingredients:

l 1 cup stemmed and sliced strawberries

l 1 cup of sliced cucumbers l A pitcher of cold water

Directions:

1. Add all the fruit to the pitcher of water.

2. Stir well to incorporate the flavors.

3. Refrigerated for at least two hours to allow the fruit flavor to infuse the water.

Strain and serve chilled. This can be refrigerated up to two days.

Grapefruit Water

Time: 5 minutes

Serving Size: 6

Ingredients:

l 1 cup of fresh squeezed grapefruit juice

l A pitcher of cold water Directions:

4. Add the grapefruit juice to the water.

5. Refrigerate and serve chilled.

Black Lemon Iced Tea

Time: 5 minutes

Serving Size: 6

Ingredients:

l 6 cups water

l 3 black tea bags

l ½ cup of stevia

l ¼ cup orange juice

l ¼ cup lemon juice

l Fresh mint leaves

Directions:

1. Bring three cups of water to a boil over medium heat in a large saucepan. Remove from the heat and steep the tea bag for five minutes.

2. Remove the tea bags and discard.

3. Move the tea to a large pitcher and add the remaining ingredients.

4. Refrigerate and served chilled. Garnish with mint.

Raspberries Iced Tea

Time: 15 minutes

Serving Size: 8

Ingredients:

l 3 cups fresh raspberries

l ¼ cup of stevia l 1 tablespoon chopped fresh mint

l A pinch of baking soda

l 4 cups boiling water

l 2 green tea bags

Directions:

1. Combine raspberries and stevia in large bowl. Crush the mixture with wooden spoon.

2. Add the mint and baking soda. mix and set aside.

3. Steep the tea bags in boiling water. cover and let stand three minutes then remove and Discard the tea bags.

4. Pour green tea over raspberry mixture and let stand at room temperature for at least an hour. Strain the raspberry tea and served chilled.

Chamomile Orange Iced Tea

Time: 10 minutes

Serving Size: 8

Ingredients:

l 8 chamomile tea bags

l 12 cups of boiling water

l 1 cup of orange juice

l 4 teaspoons stevia

Directions:

1. Steep the tea bags in boiling water for five minutes.

2. Remove and discard the tea back and allow the tea to cool completely before adding the remaining ingredients. Stir to mix. 3. Refrigerate and serve chilled or with ice.

Mint Tea

Time: 10 minutes

Serving Size: 5

Ingredients:

l 5 cups of boiling water

l 2 green tea bags

l 6 mint leaves

l 4 teaspoons stevia

Directions:

1. Steep the tea bags in boiling water for five minutes.

2. Remove and discard the tea back and allow the tea to cool completely before adding the remaining ingredients. Stir to mix. 3. Strain and serve immediately. This can be refrigerated and served chilled.

Basil Ginger Tea

Time: 15 minutes

Serving Size: 2

Ingredients:

l 3 large basil leaves

l ½ teaspoon of finely grated ginger

l Boiled water

Directions:

1. Add all the ingredients to a teapot and brew until it reached your desired strength.

2. Sieve the basil and ginger, and serve

3. This beverage can be served cold by adding ice or refrigerating.

Green Veggie Juice

Time: 5 minutes

Serving Size: 2

Ingredients:

I 4 celery stalks

I ½ cup of diced cucumber

I 1 cup of diced pineapple

I ½ cup of diced green apple

I 1 cup of washed spinach

I 1 lemon

I ¼ cup of sliced ginger

Directions:

3. Add all the ingredients to a juicer and juice.

4. Consume the juice immediately.

Pineapple Juice

Time: 10 minutes

Serving Size: 2

Ingredients:

I 2 cups of cubed pineapple

I 1 cup of water

I ½ inch of ginger

I ½ teaspoon of salt

I 3 basil leaves

I 1 tablespoon of lemon juice

Directions:

1. Add all the ingredients to a blender and blend until smooth.

2. Strain to remove solid bit and serve immediately. Can be served with ice.

CONCLUSION

Although the anti-inflammatory diet is generally good for health, it is especially suitable for treating some health problems. For example, the anti-inflammatory diet reduces the risk of heart disease, keeps existing heart problems under control, reduces blood pressure and triglycerides in the blood (natural fats formed by the combination of fatty acids and glycerol) and soothes hard rheumatic joints.

This diet aims to increase physical and mental health by recommending healthy, fat, fiber-rich fruits and vegetables, abundant water, and a limited amount of animal protein (excluding fish), providing a constant source of energy and reducing the risk of age-related diseases.

Good luck!

CPSIA information can be obtained
at www.ICGtesting.com
Printed in the USA
LVHW010132220221
679513LV00002B/106